RATTLED AWAKE

Volume Five

Rattled Awake
Anthology Authors

Lonnee Rey

CONTENTS

INTRODUCTION

Our intention is to help you move through the challenges of our ever-changing world..and do it with ease.

From conscious parenting and creating legacies, personal and professional pivots, to preparedness packing and fighting for freedom, these authors are on a roll, excited to share *Rattled Awake* insights that will help you in ways you are sure to find both inspiring and motivating.

Enjoy this, the fifth in an ongoing series dedicated to raising the voices of ordinary people doing extraordinary things in unprecedented times.

It's amazing what you can do when
you don't know you can't.

SHAKEN FROM THE DARKNESS...ROBB PROFANCIK

When growing up, did you ever envision yourself building a beautiful life, just to throw it all the way in the blink of an eye? NO?! Well, neither did I, but that's exactly what I did.

I loved living life with a caring family, 'ride or die' friends and developed deep, meaningful relationships with others. I was so like my mother, where she cared very much about others. She would do anything for someone without giving it a second thought. I developed her traits as I got older. Doing this gained me the respect of my friends, family and others. The only thing missing was my confidence to speak freely and openly to anyone. If I didn't know you, then my silence took a front seat to a social interaction. I only spoke when someone initiated a response from me. I kept my opinions and my ideas to myself. Hell, I even kept my emotions to myself, even to those that mattered to me the most. This was typically with girlfriends and significant others mostly. By not talking, I was considered 'stuck up' or 'too good for others.' By all means, this was so far from the truth. I struggled meeting new people, especially girls at the time. I accepted this, defeatedly, and continued on.

As I got older, I started working in a marketing firm after high school. Here I developed a rapport of being well liked and at times invited out for drinks after work with a group of coworkers. Here is where the awkwardness started. I didn't engage in conversation, rather I sat silent, listening and observing. Then, at one outing I decided to have a beer and a couple more. Guess what? I found my power to speak and the flood gates were opened. Oh boy, did they ever! I was engaging, laughing and everything I hoped I could do before. Alcohol was my answer…my liquid courage.

You might be asking yourself, 'Yeah, so!? I have a couple to loosen up too.' You're right! But what you didn't do is rely on it so much that it began to control your life. Granted, this didn't happen overnight. It was a little over a year before the change took place. I found myself not just having a couple, when we went out after work, but eventually wanting more after I went home. This went on for a few years. In that time, I created rifts in my family, lost close friends, due to alcohol. C'mon! How many times are they going to drive me home because I was too wasted to drive or end a night early because I was too belligerent? Yeah, not too many.

Losing friends, missing family gatherings and sometimes missing work, all because I was too drunk or hungover. *THE BOTTLE FINALLY WON!!*

Not so fast…one day on December 30, 2001, I finally realized I was throwing my life away and put down the drink after partying hard for a few years. Unfortunately, I didn't set it down for good. I stayed sober for 5 years and I was living a great life with a loving girlfriend and my family back to supporting me.

One day I thought to myself that I could have a couple. I

just need to stay away from the bars and nightclubs. So, I decided to drink at home, but just on the weekends. I did just that for a while and drank responsibly...until I didn't.

As time went on, I started adding a day here and a day there, until I was drinking every night after work. Let's just say that, by this time, my demon had his arm around me and said, "Welcome back!"

This time he didn't let me out of his sight. He robbed me of so many things. He shook the foundation of my family... AGAIN! Completely shook the foundation of my confidence and my worthiness. The confidence and worthiness I gained through this asshole of a demon named alcohol. I just went to work and came home and drank. Luckily, I didn't succumb to drinking before work or during, just after.

Then the darkness came. My mind, body and soul were not mine anymore. My demon took sole custody of me and his claws were unmerciful. My life, as I knew it, was gone and the solitude was deafening. The constant noise in my head drove me insane, yet there was no one around. My dreams and desires were nonexistent and I could care less. The only thing I cared about was that next drink, that next escape.

Needless to say, my demon allowed me to keep one thing as my own. He allowed me to keep my determination to go to work every day. The one thing I still excelled at and the only thing I was proud of. Everything else was a pure shitshow and I just sank and sank into a bottomless depression, where I never thought I would come out of. Outside of work, there were three things that my life consisted of: vodka, sofa and TV.

My family saw right through my lies and excuses, but never gave up on me. I used people for my selfish needs and never had a care in the world if this hurt them. I used family, friends (the ones that stuck around) and women. You name it, all for my own satisfaction. One person in particular I severely used was a truly beautiful and wonderful woman. She had a heart of gold and a heart full of love to match. Unfortunately, she became an emotional hostage as I played on her emotions for my selfish benefit. I won't go into details, but you can imagine what developed between us. Did I do this because I loved her? NO! I did it solely because my deprived alcohol thinking wanted to cause mayhem in another person's life. One important point is that she was married and not happy in her marriage. This gave me the perfect out! I can walk away anytime I wanted…and I did. I eventually ended up ghosting her and never answering and never contacting her. Am I ashamed of this? Yes, I truly am today and hopefully one day I can find her, make my amends to her and let her know how truly sorry I am for having done this.

This is not the type of person I used to be nor who the sober me was. I have always been loyal and trustworthy to everyone, especially girlfriends and women in my life. What I did was diabolical; I was deep in my alcoholic addiction.

Why am I telling you this? As a reminder that I never want to be this person again. It's hard to admit this and I have to verbalize this with you, the reader, and others. That way I will always know that picking up my next drink will not only hurt me, but hurt many other people as well. Just like the woman I had no regard for. God, I truly hope I find her.

All of this just created more and more of my self-loathing and self-pity. I always reached for my answer to cure my ills, which was alcohol.

There was a point where I got laid off, because my company was shutting down the warehouse where I was working. They offered me another position at one of their other facilities, but I declined. This was too far of a drive and meant I had to get up earlier to go to work. How dare they think that they could interfere with my nightly drinking!! I wouldn't allow it, or should I say that my demon wouldn't allow it.

So, I was laid off and figured I'd take a few weeks before finding another job. What the heck, the severance package was awesome and I had plenty of money to drink and didn't have to worry about getting up to go to work. I was set. Or so I thought...This new found free time just opened my portal to darkness even more. Instead of anticipating a drink after work, I started drinking as soon as I woke up, whenever that was. I figured I had nothing better to do, might as well keep the numbness going and try escaping from this depression.

Man, was I so wrong. My depression became worse and more severe. My thoughts drastically changed to thoughts of deep darkness and despair. My mind was racing with terrible thoughts. Thoughts that the sober me would NEVER create.

This weighed on me for some time and the only release was to put it down on paper, so I wrote it in a story. I could not believe that I could even bring myself to write something as awful as this, but it was the only thing I could do to try and eradicate this from my mind. Now mind you, this is totally something I would never do...sober or drunk...but I was ashamed that my addiction brought me this far.

SANITY HEARS "IN" KNOCKING

My world is less complex than most,

But to stop moving, I would be toast
-

I keep up with the rat race and the Dow Jones every day,
Hoping to save enough to pay the monthly bills, I pray.
-

Things happen...things break...loans are paid off...so to speak,
A moment taken to realize my monetary status...IT'S PEAKED!
-

What to do? When my employment pays barely peanuts,
Should I freak...hoping not to go COMPLETELY NUTS!
-

With everything in disarray, I contemplate my next move,
Wishing that my current monetary gig has more to prove.
-

I've done all I can do to compensate for my monetary woes,
Desperately imploring my banker with an attitude of "Anything Goes!".
-

He conveyed a horrific story, never to be heard again,
Because I run out, with a tantrum like I was 10.
-

I run...hearing knocking here and there; again hearing the same,
Gotta hold tight, I've been there before and know the game.
-

I stop and shout, "WHAT DO YOU WANT?", and the words fall like rain,
I succumb to the knocking; I yield to "IN and find INSANE!!!!!!!!!
-

My sanity has merged with "IN", unbeknownst to me; I'm

uneasy,
There are things I'm ordered to do, but I'm feeling very queasy.
-

What is this? What is making me do something I do not want to do?
Viciously I fight this "alien" intrusion and hope we are through.
-

Instantly, I feel the urge to do things I don't do daily,
And find myself with my hands full, choking an individual gaily.
-

With no disregard for human existence, I went along my route,
A biker came up to me and for no reason, I punched him out.
-

I assessed what happened; I realized "IN" has influenced me,
Wanting myself back wasn't going to happen, with me an enlistee.
-

Out of my mind, I called out to "IN", "WHAT THE FUCKING HELL?"
"Why join forces with my sanity to commit these actions?" ..." WELL?"
-

After a brief silence, a rumbling came I could barely recall,
It said, "YOU CAME TO ME TO RECTIFY YOUR LOSSES AND DEMOLISH ALL!"
-

Out of it I asked quizzically, "When did THIS take place?"

"It was a time when YOU needed "IN" ...a time of GREAT DISGRACE!"

-

"I NEVER ASKED FOR YOU! I ASKED GOD FOR HELP IN MY NEED!"
"'IN' comes when called upon, deep down you prayed for my creed!"

-

Confused, I said, "HOW DID I ASK FOR YOU, WHEN WANTING GOD?"
Waiting for a response, I screamed again...NOTHING. VERY ODD!

-

With no answers, I return to a family not at home,
Everyone is out; I retire, and only worry about the beer foam.

-

No one to interrupt my solace, I watch some sports on the tube,
I hear a knock on the door, cooling my beer with the last ice cube.

-

Opening the door, the POLICE are here questioning of a killing,
Frantically I let them in and I find the result very chilling!

-

"This involves me?" ...but before I could finish, I'm on the ground,
WHY?" comprehending, then hear, "You've FINALLY BEEN FOUND!"

-

I struggle to find answers quickly, but find my face in mud!
"Murderer!!! Your hands have you're family's blood!"

-

I recollect what I had done previously...AND I AM
SHOCKED!!!!!!!!!!
I've done something I would NEVER DO...then hear the cell
door Locked!

-

In my 9x10 solitude, I wonder WHAT THE FUCK
HAPPENED...AND MORE!!!!
Did I kill MY FAMILY! space out and commit a crime only to
ignore!

-

I DIDN'T DO IT! I would scream; reality & acceptance can't
coincide,
Searching for answers, I find that my memory has lied.

-

I've succumbed to "IN"; fully not knowing what's
transpired all night,
Murdering dreams...not my family, but now think they
may be right.

-

Confined makes one think; I cry out to "IN", "PLEASE
HELP!"
Gaining enough courage; "I'M INNOCENT!", barely I yelp.

-

Everything shakes, then... "YOU GOT WHAT YOU PRAYED
FOR, OKAY?",
"I PRAY TO GOD FOR MY NEEDS". Oh Shit, was it to GOD? I
pray....

-

In my solitude, I realize to whom I prayed the entire time,
During my chaotic state, I TRULY asked for a partner in crime.

-

Now I know what my partner IS…I prayed to the wrong side,
I wanted SO MUCH and was swayed by the opposite guide.

-

Today is court, and I'm truly positive I can plead my case,
As proceedings go, my memory surfaces, which I embrace.

-

Psychotically I feel myself stabbing and killing people numerously,
Thinking, as the judge asks for my opinion, I respond humorously.

-

Seeing my actions and his retort, I'm held in contempt…for good,
He hereby declares me clinically insane, which he definitely should.

-

Fully snapped, I assess what happened…I know one thing,
I WILL KILL ANYONE, ANYWHERE, FOR I AM THE "IN" KING!!!!

-

I stated this non-stop for hours…day in…day out…again and again,
"I KILLED THEM, YOU KNOW? YOU KNOW I'M NOT SANE????

-

"FUCK SHOCK THERAPY, IT REMINDS ME WHAT I DID TO

MARY,

I stuck one end of an electrical cord in water;...IT WAS SCARY!!!!!!

-

TO HELL with Mary...it's what I did to the kids that makes it worthwhile,

I yelled at them and sent them to Grandma's...See, I'm not that vile.

-

In my permanent abode; hands tied behind my back; it's VERY WHITE!

Strangely bound tight, but am complacent in "IN's" world that's just right.

-

Time for medicine...I take like a champ...which is more than most,

I (heh, heh) ...stop moving...like most (heh, heh) ...mm mm... LOVES toast.

(This was a short story that I wrote on January 26, 2009. This was written in my deepest, darkest depression. My thoughts were dark and I was completely drunk when writing this. This goes to show you how dark someone can go in their alcoholism or addiction. These were just thoughts and never was to be acted out at all. Just needed to write this out to get it out of my head.)

(PHOTO IS A SCULPTURE BY: THOMAS LEROOY
TITLED, "FIRST THE MAN TAKES THE DRINK, THEN
THE DRINK TAKES THE MAN." (2014)

Now my drinking was full-blown out of control. Every waking moment I had to have a drink. During this time, I was always drunk and too incapacitated to drive to the neighborhood store, so I started to have my alcohol delivered to me.

By this time, I wasn't drinking beer, but straight vodka and lots of it. The effect was fast and swift and kept my mind diluted and numb. After doing this for over a month, something happened to me that has never happened during my years of drinking. I started to develop "the shakes" or DTs (delirium tremens), as some call it. This scared the hell out of me and the only way to make them go away was to drink more alcohol. Not only was I drinking to escape my depression, now I HAD to drink to make myself feel semi-normal. WHAT THE FLIPPIN' HELL IS HAPPENING TO ME????

My shakes gave me severe heart palpitations and scary, labored breathing. It felt like I just ran around the block twice, but I was sitting on my sofa as I've done that past month and a half. I was now terrified and thought I was going to die. (Sadly, during this long binge drinking, I thought to myself how relieving it would be to never wake up and end this nightmare once and for all.) Now I wanted to LIVE!!! I DID want to wake up now and I didn't want to die!!

One late morning I was woken up by these shakes and they were so severe that I didn't think I was going to make it through the day. I had to do something and I had to do it NOW!! Right then I had the rattled awake moment and decided…I'm DONE! I need help! I called my brother, hoping he would answer my call. Please pick up! PLEASE PICK UP! "Hello." was on the other end…THANK YOU GOD!

I told my brother that I'm in bad shape and I desperately need help. I told him about the constant shake and the racing heart, etc. He said, "Do you have any more alcohol?" I said I did. He instructed me to drink as much as I needed to calm myself down and he'll call me right back. He called me back about 20 minutes later and said I can be admitted to a local detox center called Stella Maris, but not until Sunday morning. It was Saturday morning I called, so I endured this for almost another 24 hours.

I had to find a way to put the pieces of my life back together, because my addiction was making me feel worthless and invaluable as a human being.

Finally, the day arrived and he was there first thing in the morning to drive me to the detox center. As I walked through those glass doors, I felt a sense of calmness I hadn't felt in quite some time. I surrendered myself and reached out for help, the help I so desperately needed.

After five days in detox, I was informed I would receive a spot in a local rehab center called The Lantern. Here I began to transform to a new version of my old self, without alcohol. I never realized that it wasn't the old me, rather a BRAND NEW me I was being transformed into.

I was introduced to the program of Alcoholics Anonymous (AA) and I was so ready to take in everything they had to offer. I wanted badly to separate myself from the darkness and demon that had total control of my life for so long. This was just what I desperately needed. The AA program taught me to love myself again and to truly live a fulfilling life. They based their program on the 12 Suggested Steps of Alcoholics Anonymous. Within these steps, they emphasize the importance of surrendering from your addiction, finding a power greater than ourselves (Higher Power or God) that could restore our sanity and then turning our will and lives over to that Higher Power.

For me, I already believed in God and thought He had forsaken me in my darkness, but now come to know that He was always there with His hand outstretched. I was the one who needed to be willing to reach up and grab His hand. These are the Steps I was instructed with to live a fulfilling life I always wanted:

    1. We admitted we were powerless over alcohol.

That our lives had become unmanageable.

2. Came to believe that a Power greater than ourselves could restore us to sanity.

3. Made a decision to turn our will and our lives over to the care of God (Higher Power) as we understood Him.

4. Made a searching and fearless moral inventory of ourselves.

5. Admitted to God (Higher Power), to ourselves and to another human being the exact nature of our wrongs.

6. Were entirely ready to have God (Higher Power) remove all these defects of character.

7. Humbly asked Him to remove our shortcomings.

8. Made a list of all persons we had harmed, and became willing to make amends to them all.

9. Made direct amends to such people whenever possible, except when to do so would injure them or others.

10. Continued to take personal inventory and when we were wrong promptly admitted it.

11. Sought through prayer and meditation to improve our conscious contact with God (Higher Power) as we understood Him – Praying only for knowledge of His will for us and the power to carry that out.

> 12. Having had a spiritual awakening as the result of these steps, we tried to carry this message to alcoholics, and to practice these principles in all our affairs.

(These steps are courtesy of the AA Big Book written by Bill Wilson and originally published in 1939.)

These steps not only can be used by those coming out of active addiction, these can be incorporated in the everyday lives of just about anyone. Come to think of it, I just may interpret these steps for everyday people and put them on paper. The 12 Steps to Living a Fulfilling Life.

I am just one of many where the AA program has worked wonders for my healing and keeping my sobriety. I know there are some reading this that aren't too keen on AA, because it's spiritual-based. To fully heal and conquer your demons, you must have some spiritual guidance or Higher Power to guide you. Whether it be the universe or anything you truly believe in. Also, support is absolutely necessary, because doing this on your own is not impossible, but way harder than it needs to be.

There are people, places and organizations out there just willing to help you on your road to recovery. No one can make you choose this path. This is entirely up to you. Don't you want to choose a better way of life? A more fulfilling and freeing life? I know you do!

If the one reading this is not in active addiction and has someone that is, then please don't give up on them. They are not who they once were. Keep tabs on them from a distance, so that you are there once they are willing and able to get the help they so desperately need. They are trapped deep in the darkness and they are trying like hell to get out. Believe me…I was one of them.

Today I am living proof that you can live a truly wonderful life with promise and with goals. Sobriety is my No. 1 priority now and I protect it to the fullest extent. Let's just say that I protect it with the vigor and tenacity that I used in obtaining my next drink while in active addiction…and I would do just about anything to do that!

My demons will always be a stone's throw away and I don't want to go "toe to toe" with them ever again. That's why I promise myself not to drink *just for today.* If you take it One Day At A Time, you definitely can make this a reality!

I am active in the AA program, where I attend weekly meetings at least three times a week. I have a sponsor (mentor) who leads me through the steps and guides me in my sobriety. I also sponsor others the same way. Not only am I sober now, I give back and help others achieve and maintain sobriety.

I hope that my story has given one person hope that it is possible to break free from the chains of addiction. If you are reading this and not in active addiction, please know there is always hope that someone you know will CHOOSE LIFE!

There is light at the end of that dreary, dark tunnel…a truly BEAUTIFUL LIGHT!!

I leave you with this. What are you willing to do to escape the darkness?

LINKS:

www.alcoholicsanonymous.com
www.aa.org
www.samhsa.gov
www.findtreatment.gov
www.britelife.com

SAMHSA National Helpline:
1-800-662-4357

Robb Profancik is on a mission to spread hope and positivity wherever he goes. Letting others know that the darkness is not permanent and brighter days are right around the corner.

By day he is a machine assembler at Kiffer Industries, Inc. and by night he gives others hope, inspiration and encouragement with his amazing daily quotes he posts on LinkedIn.

His posts can be found right here on his LinkedIn profile:

Robb Profancik - Machine Assembler at Kiffer Industries Inc - Kiffer Industries Inc | LinkedIn

Robb has been sober for over 2 and a half years and helps those struggling with addiction whenever he can, so that they can live the beautiful life he is living today!

He is active in the AA program and fellowship where he has a sponsor (mentor) and also sponsors others to achieve and maintain sobriety.

I NEVER WANTED TO BE A MOTHER… LISA MARREE

Who and what you resist the most, is often your greatest teacher - Lisa Marree

"Hi Lisa, please take a seat."

The receptionist knew me well. I had sat in that waiting room dozens of times.

It was so ironic that the women surrounding me were there for fertility treatment, so desperate to have a baby and I was completely the opposite.

I could see the anxiety and sadness in their faces knowing that this round of IVF may not be successful.

 I was sick, angry and in so much pain that I just wanted it to all end.

Today was the day I was going to change all that.

I had made up my mind I was going in there to demand a hysterectomy. I had rehearsed several times what I was going to tell the doctor and he was not going to change my mind.

I was 29, had been prodded, poked, chopped up dozens of times, injected and ingested horrible pharmaceuticals and hormones and yet my health was so bad AND declining, there was no end in sight.

The last straw was the two-week spiral into chemically-induced menopause, which was a six-month treatment to stop my pituitary gland from producing the important sex hormones a young person required, not just for making babies, but the important role in bone density, heart health, metabolism, nervous system regulation, hair, nails, collagen production…

Most people do not understand the systemic effect of menopause! These are vital hormones for the whole body!!

It wasn't just about the bio-physiology effects… it made me feel PSYCHOTIC! It was horrible, uncontrolled mood swings that were exacerbated by the insomnia. Menopause is NO joke, and I was only 29!!!

I had aggressive systemic endometriosis that triggered multiple other autoimmune conditions. How 'interesting' that my most diseased part of my body was my reproductive system. Stop to think about that phenomena for a moment, how deep deep emotional trauma can 'target' disease in a certain area of your body.

Have you ever heard "thought's become things"? Hmmmm fascinating huh!

"Lisa."

Dr. A. called me in.

"Take a seat."

My heart was pumping and I could feel the tension through my body knowing that he was not going to be happy with what I was about to tell him.

"How are you?"

"I've had enough, I want a hysterectomy."

He looked over the top of his glasses and put his pen down and said "I'm not prepared to do that, you're too young and we know that in some cases if you have a baby the disease will correct itself."

"I don't want to have children and I can't deal with this anymore."

I felt his resistance and I was ready for the challenge.

"Lisa, I've had too many women come back to me five or ten years later crying because they were ready to have a baby. This is final and you can't go back."

I could feel the rage building inside of me, trying so hard not to cry.

"Nothing has worked and I'm having two operations a year. I feel sick all the time. I'm in so much pain and I've had enough. If you don't do it I will find a doctor who will."

"I really don't think you're thinking clearly at the moment Lisa. Before I even consider this, I need you to take a psychological assessment and I want your husband to be part of it as well. The decision just should not be yours in a marriage."

Of course I wasn't f*cking thinking clearly BUT I was

definitely sound of mind. And I did not need my narcissistic husband who also didn't want children to be part of 'my body' decision making.

I played the doctor's game and went through the Psychological assessment with my husband. I made it very clear to the Psychologist that I would definitely become psychotic if I don't have a hysterectomy.

I was really pissed off. WHY is it 'expected' that just because I am female, I want to have a baby?

If you don't feel it, WHY bring a child into the world?

I certainly convinced the Psychologist, in fact I think she was a bit scared of me! LOL..

It was surgery day and I'm sitting in the pre-op room waiting for the anesthetist to discuss the usual drug regime.

The door opened and Dr A. walked in and looked at me with a combination of pity, frustration and compassion in his eyes, then asked me one more time "Lisa this is final. Are you absolutely certain you want to go through with this?" One word. "*YES.*"

Lying in the operating theatre for the 13th time I had a sense of relief. I knew the next couple of months was going to be pretty uncomfortable but I was looking forward to not having to go through this again.

Well… it wasn't the last time I had surgery, I'm up to 18 times now. The years of fear created catastrophic health problems. My body is a living example of the long-term effects of stress. I did find my own solutions, but that is for another time.

Life moved on from my second husband. I made another bold decision to walk away with nothing but a suitcase and a $500,000 debt and facing bankruptcy. I was 33.

The short back story here... as a young naive person regarding business I had so much to learn. I willingly went guarantor with my two investment properties for him so he could buy a small catering business. The bank encouraged this course of action, over inflated the prices of my properties that I had to re-mortgage for almost double the value. You know how the story goes, the business went broke and I had the debt.

Along comes Brad.

Brad had not long come out of his own relationship. The chemistry was amazing and things got pretty serious pretty fast.

There was a slight complication. Brad had two girls under the age of three.

Oh boy... this is a BIG deal!

ZERO... no... in fact BELOW ZERO interest or maternal instincts existed in my body or mind.

You're probably wondering at this stage why I do not have a maternal cell in my body. Here's a snapshot of that story...

My childhood was one of fear and survival. My mother had a violent psychiatric illness and was in and out of psychiatric wards throughout my childhood.

Constantly being told "I wish I never had you," "you've ruined my life" and "I wish you were dead" probably had some impact!

That was just the verbal abuse and emotional blackmail. The physical violence was brutal and often more than punching and kicking; there were knives and other things.

I think I was around six or seven when my mother remarried. My father got out of there when I was four. That's a whole other story… but the cruel fact was he did not take us with him.

My mother was highly intelligent with her 'Borderline Personality Disorder,' and convinced all of the authorities that my father was the offender in the custody battle.

My 'new dad' was a Vietnam veteran infantry soldier who lived each day drinking himself to sleep.

He was no help or support, and didn't protect us from mother's crazed attacks because he got attacked, too!

I was a withdrawn, scared, quiet observer of this heinous life I lived and witnessed.

I was never held.

I watched my mother lie and talk about other people in such a venomous way.

I did not learn about values.

I was not encouraged to be independent; the control she had on my sister and I was terrifying for us to not comply.

We dare not show our emotions …. that triggered a frenzy.

"Safety and security don't just happen, they are the result of collective consensus and public investment. We owe our children, the most vulnerable citizens in our society, a life free of violence and fear." — Nelson Mandela

My childhood was just surreal, almost watching it all happen as though I was watching a movie and I was not connected to myself.

Do you ever stop to think how your own upbringing has impacted your parenting or how you treat children?

This is a huge question.

How do you greet your children?

How present are you when you are in playtime with your children, or talking with them?

Is your discipline positive discipline or negative discipline?

Do you hear yourself saying ALL OF THE TIME, don't do this, be quiet, I'm too busy, don't touch that, hurry up, why don't you listen?

If you are having a bad day does that spill over into how you speak to and treat your children?

I will sprinkle some other self-assessing questions a little later on.

WHY am I asking these questions?

It will be revealed soon, so hang in there with me!

I am now in my 50s and have spent many years undoing the layers that were imposed upon me in my impressionable years.

I was a runaway teenager and stupidly went back after the police convinced me that it would be okay. I was so withdrawn, emotionless and disconnected that all I could do was finish my final year at high school and was the first intake into the military the following year.

I was out!

I grew up as a lone wolf.

Driven for success (aka significance and self-worth), and I was out to prove it no matter what. I remember even being called an "Ice Maiden" … oof.

An injury took me out of the military, so I then went to university and became a Medical Scientist. That's where I worked my butt off and got my two investment properties…the ones I handed my ex-husband on a silver platter!

You get the picture now… So, let's get back to Brad.

This is where I became an entrepreneur, in 2004. That decision CHANGED MY LIFE.

This is not the chapter where I dive into how I became a six-figure entrepreneur in Holistic Health & Business Coaching. You will find the roller coaster fail-success story and my mission in the International Best Selling "Rattled Awake Volume 3."

My message in this chapter is to Rattle Awake '**Conscious Parenting**'.

What is Conscious Parenting? I'll get to that shortly.

So by the age of 33, I had not changed a nappy (diaper), done any 'Nanny' duties, did not go to baby showers and definitely wasn't in the circle of pass the cute baby around and have a hold. In fact, if any doting mother asked did I want to 'hold' the baby, my insides seized up and it was an immediate "no thanks".

Why do people want to hold someone else's baby? I was totally intrigued, but not tempted.

Let's not even start the conversation about "have you got any kids?" or "do you want to have children". It was an easy answer for me post hysterectomy. *"No, I had a hysterectomy due to endo."*

The looks of pity I got and the "oh I'm so sorry" was annoying, but I played along and said "it's ok, there were too many medical complications. I'm ok with that. I have nieces and nephews.

"Maybe you can adopt" … it was never ending!!

Back to my boyfriend who is a single dad of 2 infant girls.

Well…. we moved in together.

The arrangement was a 50/50 share care. Mikaela & Madison had Wednesday - Sat/Sunday with Brad…. with … us.

My walls were up, and I made it very clear I was NOT going to take the role of their mother. That's her job!

My insides felt like a roller coaster, half the week I could be myself, the other half of the week I was internally in lock down. I felt like a grumpy matron, not engaging in conversation, but doing house duties of what felt like a 'care-taker' role. That is what I decided would be the best step mother role I could be at this point in time.

When the girls started school, I did do not drop off or pick up, I did not assist with homework, I did not take them to after school activities, I did not read them bedtime stories, I did not tuck them into bed, I did not organise their birthday parties, Brad did all that.

Brad was and is still an incredible father and friend to the girls.

He was also physically beaten, what he recalls as every day, by his father's hand. For Brad to be a good father he said all he had to do was flip it 180 degrees of how his father treated him.

He was emotionless just like me, and a hardass just like me, but his girls were and are his everything. I believe they are the reason he is still alive today.

There is NO excuse, you CAN break the cycle. GET HELP! WAKE UP! Don't f*ck up your children because you are hurting!

"It is easier to build strong children than to repair broken men."
— Frederick Douglass

Each day, I felt like a broken record and heard myself saying…

"Can you set the table please… can you make your bed please …can you pick up your clothes please …can you tidy the kitchen after yourself please…can you keep the noise down please… have you done your homework… can you hurry up please, we are running late"

I virtually engaged in no other conversation. There was occasional small talk, and a daily hug before they went to bed.

While they were still quite little, under the age of 10, I found myself getting frustrated with the girls when they didn't understand something that seemed so stupidly simple and obvious, until the penny dropped when I heard a line out of the famous book and documentary "The Secret".

It went along the lines of …*we've come to this earth to collect data and experiences in this life.*

I literally had an AH-HA moment realizing that a child's brain is 'empty' of experiences and that is why they ask a thousand questions about the same thing.

So life was literally filling up our brain's database of thinking, feeling, seeing, hearing, smelling, learning, actions etc.

My childhood memories were locked in a deep dark vault along with my emotions and so I didn't remember this part.

Once the girls reached teenage years I found it a little easier to engage in conversation with them. However everything else remained the same of my role purely as a caretaker to make sure they had food, shelter and safety.

In 2019 our life dramatically changed.

I had been the good 'stepmum' in my caretaker role, but the day had come for the youngest to finish high school. Brad and I had stayed in the same location only a few kilometers away from their mother and school, so the girls were not disrupted with their education even though they lived in two houses.

Brad knew that I wanted to live near the coast and I said now that the girls have left school, I'd like to move up to the Sunshine Coast. He was very reluctant to move 100 kilometers away from the girls and I don't think he thought it was going to happen for real.

We had been together for 15 years by this stage and Brad knew that I was one of those 'woo' people that could magically manifest things.

As I sit here writing these words right now, I am on my veranda of our ocean front apartment on the Sunshine Coast #grateful 'woo' moment!

Within 18 months of having that conversation with Brad, we had renovated and sold our house and moved 100km away. The girls stayed in Brisbane with their mother, their jobs and their university study.

This transition was very difficult for Brad, but for me there was an enormous sense of relief.

I could see how difficult it was for him to have that separation from the girls even though they were only an hour's drive away, but they actually loved driving up to hang out for a couple of nights in the 'beachfront apartment'.

This separation for me was an incredibly life-changing event.

Having that real *deep soul time* of reflecting on my life, as I often did, I started to think about the rules, the boundaries, the lack of understanding of child nurturing both given and received, when all the girls wanted was to be loved and show love.

Even though I had no contact with my mother since I was 20, and it had been over 30 years since I had ANY connection with her, I had done many years of healing and learning the forgiveness process, not only for her, but giving myself the grace of forgiveness for being such an emotionless 'ice maiden' for most of my life.

I MISSED OUT ON SO MUCH LOVE!

I had come to the resolution of holding space of both forgiveness and compassion for my mother knowing that she had spent her entire life in suffering. I will never condone abuse, but my eyes now look through the lens of compassion for extreme suffering versus hatred and judgment.

Not long after we moved to the coast I asked Brad if we could sit down and have a chat. I didn't know how to start the conversation so I just blurted out "you know we've done a really sh*t job at parenting".

He looked at me with sad eyes and said "I know".

This conversation was spurred on by the girls coming to stay with us for Christmas Eve and as we opened up the beautiful handmade Christmas cards they made for us, the words inside left me both touched and confused.

Handwritten messages along the lines of..... *even though we were tough, we were wonderful Role Models, and with our entrepreneur life they understood why we held such high standards for personal development, values and ethics... and they are so grateful for guiding them to be good humans, strong and independent, and helped them believe they can dream big and achieve anything they want in life ... and they loved us very much.*

US… they said US!

I was trying to hold back tears, I don't know if they ever saw me cry.
The 'ice breaker' that created a tsunami of emotions later, was they both hugged me and said "I love you Lisa".

Tears welled up in my eyes, and for the first time EVER in my 15+ years with them, I quietly whispered back with a broken voice, "I love you too".

For the record, I have tears rolling down my cheeks writing this.

The wall came crumbling down after that weekend. It was like the key turned the lock on the door to the child within me that wanted love and wanted to give love.

That is all a child is, a bubbling bliss bomb of love and giggles.

Then adults impose all their own scars, rules and crap onto that pure soul and leave them with a whole bunch of wounds that don't belong to them!! Unfortunately the cycle for most ends up generational.

It's time to WAKE UP, world!

As I started this chapter with ***"Who and what you resist the most, is often your greatest teacher".***

The Universe, God, Source, or whoever you pray to knows what the plan is.

Clearly my opinion of not wanting to be a Mother was not what the plan was.

It didn't matter that my baby making factory was removed at 29, there were higher plans for me.

Being a Mother is who I am meant to be on a Universal level, and learning how to LOVE someone else's children has been the one of the hardest and biggest lessons and gifts of my life.

Going from a contracted emotionless shell, I now stand before you as an open-hearted Messenger to ALL, feeling unconditional love and compassion for all beings, gender, race, creed. We all breathe air and bleed red… and just want to be loved.

My Mission **beyond** my entrepreneurial mission of empowering women in business to create legacies is hard to put into words, but I'll give it a go.

I stand for equipping women to be strong, courageous and resilient in their pursuit of becoming financially independent. I believe for the majority, women are the economic engines of the world, the caretakers, the life givers and the healers.

When we heal ourselves, we can heal the world.

Financially independent, soul driven women walk differently, talk differently, do differently, make decisions differently, have endless self-love and self-worth.

Not only do these mission-driven, financially independent women ferociously pursue philanthropic projects, but lead as educators and guides for conscious parenting to ensure our future generations of children are nurtured, protected and empowered.

Before I close this chapter, let me LEAD the way with my lessons about what I believe could be valuable for you on how you can become a more conscious parent for the role you have been given to bring a child into this world.

This should apply to ALL children, not just your own flesh and blood. Children are our future!

"The greatest legacy we can leave our children is happy memories" – Og Mandino

My Conscious Parenting lessons:

1. Self-awareness: being aware of our own thoughts, emotions, and behaviors as parents. You are the adult here!! Your own belief system and experiences will influence our parenting style.

2. Mindful presence: Being fully present with our children is crucial. It means giving them our undivided attention, listening actively, and engaging in meaningful conversations to foster a deeper connection. My mentor Mr Jim Rohn said "the greatest gift you can give is the gift of your attention".

3. Emotional regulation: If you don't control your emotions, how do you expect your 'copy-cat' child to be any different? Responding calmly & empathetically will have a MUCH better outcome than an impulse reaction.

4. Positive discipline: lead with understanding and teaching rather than punishment. It involves setting clear boundaries, using natural consequences, and guiding children towards

making responsible choices. Brad was incredible in the way he sat the girls down and 'explained' why they got in trouble, then gave them a hug and told them he loved them.

5.   Empathy and compassion: It took me forty years to learn this because I never received it. Nurturing empathy and compassion in children helps them develop strong emotional intelligence. By modeling empathy ourselves, we teach them to understand and respect the feelings of others.

6.   Encouraging independence: let them make age-appropriate decisions. Brad amazing me how he would give the girls two choices (both was a win for him), but it allowed the girls to think they were making the decision, rather than being TOLD how to be, do, act. PS don't tell them they cannot wear their spiderman suit out. We all need to BE who we want to be! Let the child play, dream, be creative. It's your stuff that creates limits!

7.   Creating a nurturing environment: Don't you want to feel safe? A safe and supportive environment is essential for children's emotional well-being. Kids need routines, consistent rules, and offering a loving and nurturing atmosphere.

8.   Open communication: Brad is the poster Dad again!! He encouraged open and honest communication with the girls. He actively listened to their thoughts and feelings without judgment and provided guidance and support when needed. This prevents a child from withdrawing, and being sneaky, lying, because they don't feel 'trusted'. I

know firsthand, that was my childhood.

9. Practicing self-care: Be a Role Model for goodness sake. Practice good health, eating, hydration, fitness, sleep, emotional health. Don't live on junk food, you are not a trash bin! If you want your kid to grow up with a healthy weight, great self-esteem, and emotional wellbeing, YOU lead the way!

10. Continuous learning and growth: YOU be a student of life and personal growth! It involves being open to new ideas, seeking knowledge, and adapting our parenting approach as our children grow and change.

We cannot change the past, but we have the choice to create a better future and heal some very deep wounds.

The girls are now 23 & 24, we are best friends and love hanging out together.

I am blessed.

It is very important for me to be honest, vulnerable, value-driven and live my TRUTH. As a beautiful almost 'Hero's Journey' way to close this chapter, I recently told the girls I am sorry for my lack of connection while they were growing up, and that I am aware I could have done a much better job. They graciously replied... I have been one of their greatest teachers, and know I was extremely hurt and neglected as a child, and that impacted my behavior. I will always be special because I was and always will be their mum.

To the mission-driven women who align with my message, I am sure our paths will cross in connections and collaborations as agents of change in the great awakening. Let's heal the world and create legacies together. Love and Blessings, Lisa x

Lisa Marree is on a mission to equip and upgrade purpose-driven women in transformational businesses to get visible, embody CEO level clarity, confidence, and actions, so they can bring their million-dollar ideas to life and scale to their next level in business, unapologetically thrive, doing what they love. Together we can create legacies. The world is waiting for more leaders just like you!
You can find Lisa at https://lisamarree.com

BREAK A LEG...
WENDY WISEMAN

Earlier this year I fell. It's not what you're thinking. No legs were broken in the writing or publishing of this chapter.

I've been falling for over 50 years now. As a child, as an athlete, as an actor, as a clutz, as a drunk, and yes... as a hopeless romantic, I've fallen in love more than a few times. You might say I've fallen for life.

Rough and tumble hard falling. Ripped and torn by bicycle and skateboard falls. Bruised by rugby tackle falls. Dented by a bathroom slip and fall. Broken hearted falling apart falling.

After falling do you know what to do? Get back up!

Something else I fell for: performance, as in performance art. Did you know I'm a modern dancer? Professionally trained to fall. Switched from Photography to the School of Dance in college then went to work and play in NYC. It's not a FALLacy, it's true - I've actually studied, practiced, performed and been paid to fall.

Those years of experience and exploration, that practice and training has saved me more than a few times. Physical awareness and tuning in with body sense saved me yet again earlier this year.

That F'n month!

February is cold, dark, and lonely for many people in many places. First, however, comes January commonly known as the saddest of months. This can lead to a February that may kick off 4 times as SAD if you're feeling bad. The longer you have symptoms, the worse they tend to get.

Five years fell away with that falling apart feeling. Feeling fed up. Fed up with floundering. Floundering without finding. Finding myself failing. Failing forward with that feeling of falling apart at fifty plus five.

Feeling totally F'd I fell into a deep depression and despair. I could get through shifts at work, barely, and then I'd be crying in the car driving home. Ever been there? Melancholy and malaise.

Although I never seriously contemplated doing anything dire and making no plans to commit any such act the ideations became quite consistent. That feeling of giving up. The urge to end it all.

While it's good to quit when something isn't working or doesn't feel right. It's never good to give up completely. Never give up. I didn't give up.

*** If you or someone you know is struggling or in crisis, help is available. Call or text **988** or chat **988lifeline**.org in the US ***

Ideations are ideas or concepts, often associated with problem-solving. Let's be clear here though, suicidal ideations don't solve problems. If anything, they create more problematic consequences.

Thankfully, I didn't fall for that. Even though demons of depression dragged their claws across my conscience daily. Daily I had the love of my dog. I also had my commitment to show up live for Taming Your Tension Today. These hooks pulled me through. It's important to have a big meaningful WHY to keep you on the fly.

If you read my chapter, *Grow Through,* in Volume 3 of this series you already know that this year I have been emerging from three years of grief, layers of loss and hardship. My spirits fell. I was on the edge of the deep dark well, metaphorically about to take a dive rather than choose being alive.

The show must go on.

My entire business mission revolves around choosing to be happier and healthier in each moment, come what may. Some days that means nothing more than focusing on taking another breath. And then taking another. Maybe not even getting out of bed. Being ok not being ok and knowing this will help you be better.

It was waking to the sound of my weeping housemate day after day that made my pathetic self-pity more palpable. I knew life wasn't so bad and wouldn't let myself wallow. I pushed myself up into the light.

It's heavy and hard to pull yourself up sometimes but you can do it if you put your mind to it. I would applaud myself and appreciate each tiny step.

You woke up! Good job Wendy!
You didn't wake up crying today. Good job Wendy!
You made the bed. Good job Wendy!

The morning dog snuggles are the best boost. Studies have demonstrated that petting a cat or dog can increase levels of three neurotransmitters: the feel good happiness hormones serotonin, dopamine, and oxytocin. Bringing these into better balance helps offset feelings of apathy, anxiety, or angst that can accompany depression.

Max, (dog is my co-pilot, see *Slow Your Roll* in Volume 4) is always helping me find my way. Every morning he guides me to get up and feed him! He nose all about the simple pleasures and doesn't get bogged down in the past or caught up catastrophizing the future.

{ILLUSTRATION: MICHELLE LAAKS}

Little did I know my near future would involve yet another fall.

When the weeping housemate went away on a staycation (for health not holiday) I took over the care and medication for her dogs. She has 3 senior chihuahua mix gals I like to call the 3 beans because of their bean shaped bodies. This safehold of responsibility also helped lift my spirits.

Giving and helping others is a balm for the soul.

So it was that one February day I carried my bags

toward the door to leave work and head home for the happy (hungry) dogs. The gym was unusually empty and I thought to myself, "you should put your bags down and move around on the floor" as I continued walking. Almost to the exit I said "STOP! Put your bags down and get on the floor Wendy!" (you know it's serious when you use your name, right?) and I put my bags down.

Down to the floor I went. (No, not a fall, not yet.) Floor mobility explorations are a wonderful way to loosen up, unwind, and enjoy taming your tension. Do you ever take the time to get on the floor, breathe and explore being in your body?

When I got home I wasn't as stiff as usual getting out of the car. I didn't feel quite as tired or depressed as usual either. In fact, I felt pretty darn good walking down the hallway with the dogs dancing at my feet so excited they were about to get a treat.

I turned from the hallway into the tiny hall-like bedroom entrance and hit something slick. BOOM! Down I went!

My arms shot out to each side as my left heel slid out in front of me and my foot bent back and twisted as it was shoved unnaturally under the desk monitor stand. My breath caught as I realized my other leg had bent backwards in a kind of hurdle stretch with the foot also unnaturally twisted.

Immediately I began full body sensing and scanning to offset the fears that were quickly creeping in.

✔ No dogs had been crushed.
✔ No bones seemed broken.
✔ Nothing seemed torn.

Cautiously I began to slide my foot out and unwind my twisted limbs. Ok. Before I started to rise I held each foot and used my fingers to check muscle attachments and all seemed secure if somewhat shocked.

Crawling a bit before climbing up the bed to a supported stand I completed the body scan. I was OK. Phew!

That was a close call and yet, thankfully, a catastrophe averted! The chain reaction that could have been set off there would have really dragged me into the depths of despair. Instead I was shaken out of the fuggy fog that had befallen me that F'n month.

Rattled Awake!

Sometimes it takes something alarming to shake us awake. Sometimes it takes some intense physical signaling before we wake up. Sometimes you ignore those signals, pop a pill, pull the pillow over your head, hit snooze, or smash the alarm.

Imagine if I hadn't stopped and stretched out on the floor before I walked out the door leaving work. If I had been as stiff and sluggish as usual in the evenings something likely would have been broken instead of bent.

It was 1736 when Benjamin Franklin said "An ounce of prevention is worth a pound of cure." Yet today, 287 years later, we're a society obsessed with speed and a culture consumed with quick fix cures. Why not slow down a little and focus on prevention for greater efficiency and lifelong vitality?

Had I been in better physical, mental, and emotional condition I probably would not have fallen. Had I been more tuned into being in what I was doing I probably would not have fallen. Had I been moving with greater awareness instead of with that sloppy heel strike step I probably would not have fallen.

Of course, the flip of all those add up to the other side of the coin. It could have been so much worse. If I lived a more sedentary lifestyle, my body would not have been as resilient and the fall would have been worse. If I didn't practice mindfulness, I may have had a jerky reaction of fear and the fall would have been worse. If I didn't do daily movement, my body wouldn't have been so supple and the fall would have been worse. If I didn't sleep 7-9 hours, if I didn't eat nutritiously or keep myself well hydrated my body would not have recovered so well.

WISE choices for LIFE Wendy!

Indeed, the wellness integration solution essentials of the WISE way that I developed to pull myself together when I was falling apart years prior continue to help me keep going as a happier healthier human. Creating simple health habits for integrated self-care that nurtures love, inspiration, function, essence (LIFE) promotes aging well with resilience for thriving lifelong.

HAPPIER HEALTHIER HUMANS

Get WISE for LIFE!

Simple Health Formula for Thriving Lifelong

 +  = 

FOUNDATIONS	PILLARS	RESULTS
Move	Attention	Happier
Meal	Activation	Healthier
Mind	Adaptation	Humans

Solid foundations simplify healthy living. Functional foundations support you when you fall.

We fall in so many ways throughout life.

Fall in love. Fall for it. Fall into it. Fall out. Fall overboard. Fall off the wagon. Fall off the rails. Fall asleep. Fall again. Fall back. Fall forward.

We fall repeatedly learning to sit up, crawl forward, stand up, and then walk. With every step we fall. You might say moving is falling for life.

Most injuries and accidents happen when you are

distracted, moving too fast or not physically prepared for the challenge presented. I hit all those bases on this slide at home.

My left hamstring attachment and deep hip still have some residual stickiness, adhesions of muscle tissue from that F'n fall that happened 9 months ago. Healing and realigning deeply twisted traumatized tissue takes time. We too often skip self-care in this hurry up culture of hectic living.

I see it in clients all the time. That deep seated whiplash from a fall or a fender-bender 20 years ago when they thought they were "fine" and didn't take the time to rest. Now incessantly irritating as it presents cryptic neck and back pain due to muscle guarding patterns no longer needed creating chain reactions of imbalance and chronic discomfort. The human body has incredible self-healing, regeneration and recovery capabilities if we tune in and give ourselves time.

> "PATIENCE IS THE BEST REMEDY FOR EVERY TROUBLE." —PLAUTUS

Patience is often the prevention that prevents us from becoming patients.
(Say that 10x fast - LOL!)

Paying attention usually requires some patience and if you don't pay attention you may pay a much higher price. Ever ended up in the hospital due to a momentary lapse of attention? It's costly in time, energy, and money.

Have you ever considered practices to prevent pain and injury when falling? Here you go.

Reduce the impact and prevent injury as you slip, slide, or fall with these 6 steps:

1. Protect your head.
2. Turn as you fall.
3. Keep arms and legs bent.
4. Stay soft and loose.
5. Roll through the impact.
6. Disperse the force of the fall

When you do fall - and you will fall - be sure you can get back up. Can you easily move to the floor and back up again or do you need one of the "Help, I've fallen and I can't get up" beepers? If you fall 7 times, will you get up 8?

FALL SEVEN, RISE EIGHT

七転び八起き

(nana korobi ya oki)

That's right, the Japanese proverb "Nana korobi ya oki" (seven fall eight rise) says it all.

To learn to stand, you learn to fall until you can stand on your own two feet. Once you can stand you can move on, fall forward into a step. Catch yourself and fall forward again. Fall forward building skill as you get a leg up and have a whole new perspective on overcoming obstacles. Fall for life!

Unfortunately, as you get older you forget many things, including how to fall. With all the sitting and scrolling these days most folks have forgotten how to stand. And have you seen the way people walk? Not so well, it's often more of a wobble. Even many younger adults can hardly get up off the floor when they fall.

It's one of the markers of longevity, your ability to move to the ground and rise back up without using your hands. It's a measure of muscular strength that also requires flexibility, balance, coordination and control. Can you do it?

Here's a simple test:

> [Do not attempt this test if your physical ability is compromised or there is any chance you may hurt yourself. Safety first!]
>
> 1. Stand (preferably barefoot) in non-restricting clothes with unobstructed space around you.
> 2. Cross your legs and then lower yourself to a sitting position on the floor without leaning on anything or using your hands.
> 3. Now stand back up and avoid using your hands for support.
>
> On a 10-point scale (5 points for sitting, 5 points for rising)
> > Subtract 1 point for any of the following being used for support (hand, knee, forearm, side of the leg, hand on knee/thigh).
> > Subtract 0.5 point for loss of balance.
> Total Score of 8-10 pts = You're doing great! Keep it up!

Total Score below 8 = Keep at it! You're doing great! Practice and progress!

Prepare, practice and progress. Rather than living a guarded life afraid of falling, why not build resilience by developing skill. You've probably heard "Sitting is the new smoking." It's the lack of movement, the stiffness, the stagnation that creates dis-ease. Life requires movement for there to be life

You know you need to get up, practice! You know you're going to fall, practice! Get down on it... get up and get down! Get your back up off the wall, get your butt up off the chair, get your body down on it and then rise back up off the floor!

[Take a Dance Break! Cue Music: *Get Down on It* by Kool & The Gang]

> *"How you gonna do it if you really won't take a chance*
> *By standing on the wall?"*

Get going! Do the dance! Keep Going!

Rehearsal and practice prepare you for better performance on the stage of life. You can't get anywhere if you don't step into action and start falling forward.

Awareness. Action. Adaptation.
Preparation. Practice. Performance.
Rehearsal. Risk. Resilience.

Physical resilience, mental resilience, emotional resilience and social resilience.

Rehearsal for living well. Rehearsing helps you get familiar with how you can perform at your best be that on stage, on the field, or in your life.

Practice, practice, practice 》 Progress.

Live & learn. Experience builds courage as well as capability. That's why before doing a live performance, rehearsal is crucial even if you are improvising. After all, you don't really want to break a leg! I always thought it was horrible to say that to a dancer.

Did you know that idiom came from a belief that saying good luck would actually bring about bad luck? In the Italian version the performers are hunters being wished well with "into the mouth of the wolf" and "may the wolf die" rather than "break a leg" as well wishes for a good performance.

Silly Humans.

Ask yourself, are you being a silly human about your movement, your beliefs, your fears or about falling? Have you thought about your life as a practice? Are you practicing prevention and preparedness? Maybe you're choosing to just complain and blame it on getting older.

Beware not being aware. Be aware of being in what you're doing. You're a human being after all.

How are you doing in your being? Tune in. Healthy doesn't have to be complicated. Tune in. Stop falling for all the F'n distractions and fly free. Tune in. Free yourself from frustration by falling for life.

Life is more fun when you embrace the challenges and know you're going to fall. Remember, mental rehearsals and physical practice improve performance. Get going, keep going, and en-joy the process.

L ife is moving.
Are you ready to fall for LIFE?

Wendy S Wiseman is on a mission to create a better world by taming tension and boosting vitality for busy bodies like pained professionals and GenXhausted entrepreneurs. Discover simple stress relief reminders plus a hearty dose of smiles and laughter to help you live well with less effort… get WISE with Wendy on the daily podcast, Taming Your Tension Today. En-joy MORE tips for thriving lifelong as a Happier Healthier Human when you connect with Wendy to explore coaching, courses, and the community collective at https://YAY.TamingYourTension.com

https://www.youtube.com/@tamingyourtension/podcasts

PEACE OF MIND...
LONNEE REY

Oh, the timing. I just happened to be outside at 10:30pm, and noticed some flickering orange lights through the trees. From a distance, I tried to make out if my neighbors were having a side yard bonfire. "At this hour? THERE? That's not their style," I thought to myself. I didn't hear any voices, and the orange glow was growing bigger.

Bolting down the hill from my second-story deck, it became apparent: a massive fire was building in a large pile of yard waste. Wind gusts were blowing flames within a few feet of their home. FIRE! FIRE! Flames were spreading across their lawn. Racing around to the other side of their house, I banged and *banged* on their door. FIRE!! Adam?! FIRE!! Come on!! He finally opened the door, sleepy-eyed and confused. FIRE!! It's right outside your bedroom window!

Cars slowed-down to see the blaze. "I'll call 9-1-1!" one driver said. The yard was on fire; it spread quickly and I had to jump back several times. It was so close to their home you could see soot on the house. Adam grabbed the garden hose and managed to thwart the advancing flames. It took the firemen, with full-on fire hosing, a good half hour to finally extinguish the brushfire. Whew.

"Thank you for coming over, for banging on the door like that…we were dead to the world," he said.

"Well, you *almost were* dead to the world, brother. What the hell could have caused it? That's not even your yard or pile of branches. WTH???"

He said, "Did you hear that car go by earlier? Some dude was being chased by the cops, and it sounded like he was driving on a rim. Sparks were flying everywhere."

"No. My apartment's A/C must have blocked-out the sound."

It had to be the sparks. How random is that, right? There's no telling, given the high winds that night, just how big that fire could have been, or the damage it could have caused. I was concerned that I didn't even hear a speeding car running on a rim. It made me wonder what else I'd missed…

Apartment dwellers are *especially* vulnerable to the mistakes of others. This presents a unique challenge in being prepared for anything, at any time. Regardless if it's the people, or the stuff they do, shi(f)t happens no matter what. Truth is, apartment-dweller or not, you can be severely impacted by the choices others make in life.

There are few words more terrifying than *FIRE!!*

Two years ago, a 10-alarm fire broke out at our complex. Young people were jumping off second-story balconies; older people did their best to shimmy down the square deck

supports to escape the blaze. Ouch. Meanwhile, firemen were frantically looking for fire hydrants. Apparently, no one knew the lay of the land. I couldn't believe my eyes. No one could.

Dazed residents huddled together in the parking lot. The midnight blaze robbed them of only everything. A couple of people remained calm as they phoned local hotels for a room. One woman said, "I have renter's insurance. They will cover the room while I make arrangements to restart my life somewhere." One-by-one, the remaining residents without insurance were taken to various shelters for the night. Were it not for the donated blankets and socks, their new lives would have begun as it started: barefoot and freezing cold – pajamas just didn't cut it in the 30-degree weather.

The question on everyone's mind, "How did this happen?" was a moot discussion. Asking, "Who did this?" and "Why?!" didn't change the outcome. Delete the need to understand.

The real question to be asking now is, "How fast could *you* be ready for an evacuation?"

You cannot control circumstances but you can improve your responses to curveballs.

The plandemic was one helluva curveball. Stepping back, diving headlong into rabbit holes ever since, woke me up to some harsh realities…and prompted the motto, "Don't be scared, be prepared."

I've watched thousands of hours of videos since "waking up" in 2020. A former 'sheeple' who assumed everything was fine, deep research has shown me cracks in the foundation, as co-author Chef Shawn Monroe aptly puts it. I've been Rattled Awake so big I could a write a book on the aha's and "ohh, hell naw's" discovered. Connecting the dots has formed a clear picture of what is really going on, who or what is out-and-out lying, and what we can do to be prepared if the shi(f)t hits the fan. Half of it is mental preparation; the other half is physical…literal steps you can take so you don't end-up wearing your PJs in public, too.

In this way, you can protect your peace.

Earlier this year, my hallway was filled with smoke that burned my eyes. My next-door neighbor's door was open. He smiled sheepishly, saying, "I burned the grits. It's OK now." The toxic smell told me it was more than burning grits. I ran down the hall, shouting to my elderly neighbor, Susan, "It's OK! It's OK! Stay inside!" She didn't hear me over the blaring alarm. The tangled mess of dogs, a cane and a wobbly woman made it outside. Whew. And then she fell. Two bones were sticking out of her shin. Oh. My. Goodness. There was nothing I could do but grab her purse, call her son, and wait with her until the ambulance came. Grits Guy was nowhere to be found.

Susan was gone about three months, rehabilitating that broken leg. Poor dear. Grits Guy never asked about her; never apologized for the incident. How cold can a person be? He might have a beautiful smile, but apathy is one hell of an ugly trait. I know now that it hides right underneath his spit-shine persona. When you see apathy, note it. Apathetic people care, they just don't care about you. Sound cold? Well, they are.

I thought about our neighbor, Norman, and how swiftly he strode out of the building that day. He was carrying a small suitcase in one hand; in the other, his dog on a leash. I admired his calm demeanor, loading his bag and dog into the car, then driving away. I dubbed him "Stormin' Norman" from that day forward.

Asking him about it later, he said, "There was nothing I could do that day, so I left. I've been through this before… lost everything thanks to an apartment fire 10 years ago… learned my lesson the hard way, so I always have a bag packed." Oh. Noted. It gave him peace of mind.

Stormin' Norman's experience & preparation kept him peaceful in a crisis situation. He was ready for it. That's my goal for you. Advance planning based in reality, is gold.

Norman epitomizes *"Don't be scared, be prepared."* This is my message for you today, just as it was in *Rattled Awake* volumes one and two. I have been rattled awake about food, especially after learning that over 2k food processing plant fires have occurred in the past 18 months (Vol 1). In volume two, I rang the alarm about Apeel, a toxic food coating being applied to produce, including "organic." As if that weren't bad enough, I linked to videos showing how diced ham caught fire in a microwave, along with magnetic meat, cricket flour and creepy lab-grown meat (Vol 2.) If you like to eat, and value your health, these two chapters are for you.

Rattled Awake is all about insights, epiphanies, aha's and oh-hell-no's as much as it is personal transformation and business pivots made over the last five years. When we share these stories, and solutions, everyone benefits. *Say* it forward!

Mental preparation

The people we surround ourselves with, both voluntary and inadvertently, exert influences upon us. Some are good, some, not so much.

Apathy, an especially harmful personality trait, shows up socially now, more than ever. It looks like those people who don't care enough to inquire with you, choosing instead to 'judge/jury/hang you' based on gossip. Note that, them, and this: the eyes are useless when the mind is blind. They don't want to understand. Remember, they simply do not care. And it shows. With time being our most precious commodity, it is time to move on.

Tibor has been teaching children about
love in the face of hate. Ah-mazing!

You can find our interview on YouTube.
He's sassy-sweet & inspiring!

{page 105} **"How to Deal With a Dumbass:**
What to do & say when they come your way"

Think global, act local

We have to take our power back because there are losers
posing as leaders everywhere you look these 'daze.' That is
why, in 2021, I wrote *"How to Deal with a Dumbass: what to
do and say when they come your way."* It was in response to

the global clown show on parade; and 'driven' by my then-neighbor, Kristin, who loudly pronounced "God made me a dumbass!" Believe people when they tell you who they are. It showed up in lots of ways, including the day she poured water on her oven's grease fire. It was Thanksgiving, but none of us were trying to have smoked turkey.

After that, I gave her a *huge* box of baking soda, a new can of Comet and a scrub brush. "No excuses," I thought, hoping to avert future disasters. She just laughed it off. And then it happened again: another oven fire. I knew that the Comet still had a seal on top. She'd already proven herself to be asleep at the wheel, but her apathy was truly scary, bordering on reckless endangerment.

Granted, there is only so much you can do. However, when it comes to choosing who you let in the front door, there are a few red flags to pay close attention to *before* you give them your address.

"Apathy" and "Asleep at the wheel" are two of the five red flags to look out for when assessing people. Once you are A.W.A.R.E., you can make better choices before trouble becomes your problem.

Be A.W.A.R.E. of those who exhibit one, some, or all of these traits that will trip you up:

- **A**pathetic - "couldn't care less" who they hurt in their path.

- **W**eak-willed - namby-pamby; lacking courage; "spineless wonder."

- **A**sleep at the wheel - not paying attention; lost in their own little world.

- **R**epeat offenders - these people are the definition of insanity.

- **E**rratic - someone you really can't count on.

{page 19}

"How to Deal With a Dumbass:
What to do & say when they come your way"

I get comments about my Dumbass book, like the 55-year-old man who said, "Your book helped me escape a dangerous cult in Norway." And one person literally kissed the book in praise of it, saying, "I stayed up all night reading it. In the morning, I finally freed myself from a relationship thanks to your break-up, break-out, break-free strategies."

A field guide of sorts, it's the book I wish I'd had growing up – all sorts of dramas could have been avoided. Simply put, *"Dud, stud, friend or foe? Who gets to stay and who has got to go?"* Using good judgment isn't being judgmental, it is essential.

If you enjoy podcasts instead of reading, check out the short-and-hilarious episodes on "How to Deal with a Dumbass (a spiritual perspective)" found on Spotify, Google podcasts, Stitcher, iHeart Radio, and more.

Being mentally-prepared is the backbone in protecting your peace. Today, more than ever, discernment is essential to your well-being.

Sometimes, though, we don't see it coming...

The knock at my door startled me. These days, you let somebody know you're coming over, right? "Lonnee? Lonnee?" I didn't recognize the voice and wasn't expecting company, so I didn't open the door. The voice went away.

"That was me at your door the other day. Our stove was on fire and I came over to get your help putting it out, but we got it," Christian said. Oh. Thank. Goodness.

Christian is a young professional climbing corporate ladders. He's got the GQ look, a pretty new BMW, and a bright future. But coming to my house to put out his stove fire? Not real bright, especially since he has the same fire extinguisher as me, just hanging out there on *his* kitchen wall. What was he thinking??

As they say, "common sense isn't common." Never overestimate someone's acuity based on presentation or charisma.Thank goodness we didn't have a fire that day.

Side note: Knowing his girlfriend was petrified of the dark, I gifted them three mini-flashlights. I was hoping to avert a future issue if the power went out again and candles were their idea of a good time. I wasn't so sure these two knew not to go to bed without extinguishing the flames, frankly.

"So, how's the light on those mini-flashlights?"

She said, "Oh, I don't know. We don't have any batteries." Noice.

You can lead a horse to water
but you can't make him
THINK

{page 21}

"How to Deal With a Dumbass:
What to do & say when they come your way"

Ignorance is bliss...until it isn't.

YouTube has tons of great info – training videos for just about everything. I stumbled upon The Bushcraft Prepper demonstrating stealth camping in the woods. He said, "In these circumstances, where you are stealth camping, laying low, (hiding, in other words), it is important to be quick about leaving your spot. It was 26-degrees last night and I'm freezing cold; I didn't sleep well at all. This is the perfect time, under less-than-ideal conditions, to test myself. I'm going to see if I can climb out of this sleeping bag, pack up, and be gone in under a minute." He failed on the first trial run; second time, he was done and ready to run in under a minute. Practice makes perfect.

That demonstration made me think about you: would you be able to exit your home in under a minute? A fire won't wait for you, half-asleep, bumping around in the dark, to throw a bag together. Neither will a train derailment, chemical explosions or weather events. I know, I know... what a world we live in, right? It is what it is, and it is what it ain't. Don't be scared, be prepared.

My brother, Jason, is *very* prepared...a real Macgyver-type. He is also a lifelong student of martial arts sciences, skilled with unusual self-defense weapons, such as a Katana, (long sword), and has reflexes so fast he can slice a flying Mud Dauber wasp in half with a knife. Suffice it to say, he walks through life with confidence, knowing he can handle any type of idiot.

As a Floridian, he has experienced the devastation of

hurricanes, and is fully-prepared with months of extra food, water, water filters, flashlights, and alternative power sources. Smart guy. His wife is lucky to have such a man as he: ready for anything, at any time.

Imagine my surprise when he said, "Sis, I couldn't get out of the house in a minute. I have stuff everywhere. What do you do, have a bag by the door, and an extendable ladder to get out through the window?"

Yes, and yes.

"What's in the bag? Wouldn't the type of disaster determine what you pack?" he said.

"Not really," I said. "Think of those residents who had no phone, no numbers memorized, nowhere to go, and no way to get there, Jay. I heard more than a few say their car keys were burned up in the fire, too. So, thinking in worst case scenario mode, shelter topped the list. Using a mid-size backpack, about 30L, I packed a 10x10' tarp, Wal-Mart travel hammock, paracord and bug net. This way, you and your pack are off the ground if it's raining, plus, it's light, in case you're on foot. A headlamp is more useful than a flashlight, by the way.

"You want to think in terms of building a fire, shelter, food and first aid. A small canister of butane, a pocket rocket stove, which folds up and fits into a case the size of a cigarette pack, a "Sawyer-Mini" water filter, two changes of socks, cold weather under layers, and snacks. And to access water, so I got a sillcock key."

If you don't know, a sillcock is like a wrench for outdoor faucets. If the faucet handle is missing, you can use a sillcock key. A sillcock 'clover' has four different size 'keys' (see image, right), so I recommend it to everyone.

"Yeah, Sis, I got mine at Ace Hardware. I own four; keep one in the truck, in fact." Excellent idea.

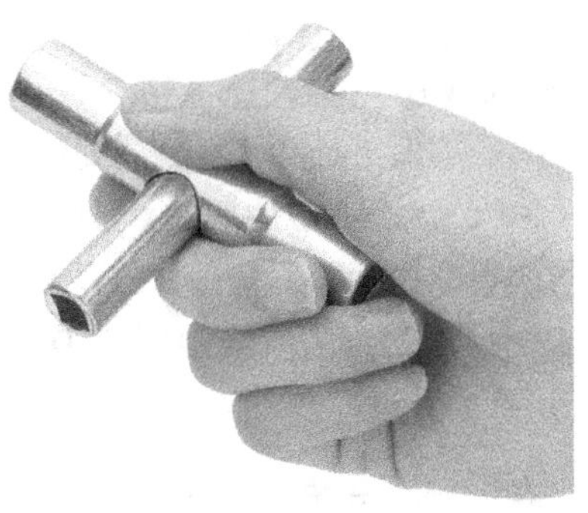

"You gotta pack your bag correctly, too, Jay, like, the first-aid kit goes on the very top of your pack. In an emergency, you'll need it fast. If you or someone else is hurt, you don't want to be digging around looking for it."

"Yeah, Sis, that makes sense...I just never thought of that...never even heard that before." Whoa. As aware and prepared as he is, this was news he could use. His first-aid kit is racked-and-stacked, tacklebox-sized and heavy. Mine is, too, but mobility means you make a smaller kit.

DutchSinse, a YouTuber who focuses on earthquakes, and, with stunning accuracy, lets the world know what to expect, when and where, (they said it couldn't be done but he's been doing it for years), is quick to point out the need for baby wipes. Dirt, dust and debris come with the territory, so pack those on top, too.

"I made a fire-starting kit, too, Jay. And this one guy showed me how to make a tiny essentials kit. Fishing line, hook, safety pins, candle, lighter, water purification tabs, sewing needle...all of it fit into an Altoids tin. I made a second one using a small, waterproof container. And man, am I glad I did all of this stuff a year or two ago." With only one good hand (I broke my wrist in two places a few months ago), there's no way I could have managed to make these kits.

"Since you might have to walk, blister pads need to be in the first aid kit. And, deciding *now* which shoes you'll wear to run out of the house will save you precious time in a pinch. Have another good pair in the car, always. Speaking of cars, you know to back-in wherever you park, right? It's faster to pull out quickly, and more accessible if you need a jump or a tow."

"Yeah, I never thought about shoes," he said. Neither did all those people in pajamas.

"What about your wallet, Sis? I mean, do you pack up everything together every night?"

If you have ever tried to replace your ID, you know you need ID to get ID. Proof of identity is the last thing you want to be fussing over as you try to use your credit card for that emergency hotel room, you know?

I said, "Well, Jay, as much as I'd like to think I've got it all together, sometimes, my ID is in a jean's pocket or purse. I need to be more organized about that. I have whittled my wallet down to three cards, all in RFID sleeves. My birth certificate, social security card, a printed list of passwords & phone numbers are all in protective page sleeves, too. Those, and a USB memory stick duplicating all that info is sitting out, on my dresser, in a zippered travel documents pouch. That way, I can grab it and go. The same thinking goes for medications: make a list and if possible have meds in one location."

Jason objected, in a way, saying, "Sis, I would have to move a bunch of things and keep them in the garage." I reminded him that 'worst case scenario' means he won't be loading up the truck, per se. "What can you fit into a backpack? How can you stay light on your feet? Imagine you have to walk, and go from there. Oh yeah, that reminds me, Jay: I also bought a silent dog repeller device after watching a trial run one guy did – he encountered dogs along the way. If things are chaotic, dogs might be on the loose. Some of those residents in the 10-alarm fire had nervous dogs in their arms because their leashes were left behind in the rush. You just never know, do you?"

Hopefully, you will never have to boogie on a moment's notice. But if you do, you won't be scared because you prepared.

Think of it as 'camping, light.' Start by making a list of what you have, or will need, to address the four main aspects: shelter, fire, food, first-aid. Dedicate three hours on a Saturday to build your 'exit, stage right' bag. Dedicate two hours to assemble vital documents and also load them onto a USB memory stick. If you bought new shoes, dedicate time to breaking them, now. You may want to spray them, as well as your chosen jacket/coat, with water repellant.

If you have a family, you can split-up the heavier items between the adults. For instance, one of you can carry food-related and fire-building, while the other can carry shelter-related. Smaller packs for the kids, with clothing basics, can also carry everyone's toothbrushes. Make it fun for the kids to prepare so they won't be scared. "Hey, kids, what can we put our clothes in to keep them dry?" One-gallon ziplock bags are ideal.

Our bodies need more water under duress. Be sure

each of you is equipped with a sturdy water bottle. This page is a terrific resource for kid-size as well as adult-size water bottles. The summary reviews will help you quickly sift through the plethora of options. https://www.verywellfit.com/water-bottles-and-carriers-for-hiking-3436082

I also wanted you to keep this in mind: my local convenience store would not sell me a bag of ice. I had cash, but they refused, saying, "Until the power comes back on, we are closed." Yikes. I was counting on them to keep food cold in my cooler. Since *that* happened, I have frozen a couple bottles of water as Plan B.

What are your Plan B's?

Thousands of residents in Philadelphia didn't know their water was about to be 'out' recently. Do you know what to do the minute an issue like that occurs, or if the power goes out unexpectedly? You have a limited supply of "good water" in the pipes and in your hot water heater. Water is *the* first thing to get stocked-up on. It's better to have it and not need it, than to need it and not have it. Make a list of 'could become a water container' and put it on the side of your refrigerator so you know exactly where to find it.

Here is what you do the minute you realize there's a power or water-related issue:

1. Line your tub with plastic sheeting, shower curtain or liner. Or, get yourself a water bladder from Amazon.

2. Fill the tub or bladder. While this is filling up:

3. Fill *everything* you can with water, then cover to protect. Suggested items: stock pots, sauce pans, pressure canner and other large containers; Tupperware, clean milk jugs, plastic tubs, bowls or bins – including plastic drawers from those inexpensive 3-drawer filing cabinets; water dispensers like beverage coolers, or filtering devices such as Zero Water; pitchers, buckets, trash cans.

4. 5-gallon containers are great because you can cover & stack them. You can also get stackable water containers (see image, below.)

5. If you have plastic storage totes, dump out the stored items, line the totes with heavy plastic then place true contractor trash bags inside; fill w/water. Invaluable, multi-purpose, true contractor bags, 3mil thick, are easy to get at Ace Hardware.

Obviously, you will need to differentiate the drinkable water from the utility water containers.

Bleach can be used to purify under most conditions. Bear in mind that bleach loses its potency over time! Yes, it actually expires. Pick up another unscented bleach next time you go shopping. The amount suggested per gallon ranges from one-eighth to one-quarter teaspoon per gallon.

Life is full of surprises – some good, some, not so much. [Recite the motto with me: *Don't be scared, be prepared.*]

More and more truth is being revealed about metals being found in tap and bottled water.

"Dre_Og Reacts" is a really informative YouTube channel. I learn so much from his curations of enlightening TikTok videos. He is also the reason I purchased a distiller.

We have all heard how pharmaceuticals pass through city water filters, right? So, given all the random Rx's being excreted, (sorry, not sorry, it is what it is), it makes sense to filter your water. I thought I was doing OK with my Zero Water filter and it's zero PPM (parts per million) filtering system.

Well, uhm…yeahhh, not so much. This close-up shows you what is left behind in my distiller whether it is tap or

"filtered" water: (look closely)

The funky white stuff and solid, chunky bits are typical residues. What is this stuff? I have no idea, mate. Was the $134 cost worth it? A million times over, if only because I drink more water now than ever before. The residue is so freaking gross, and it happens *every* time. Sadly, the Zero Water filtered water experiment also gave similar results. I am urging you to invest in your continued well-being, and in light of 'incidents' that might put you on a boil-alert.

You can find the stainless-steel DC House brand Distiller, and others, on Amazon. A gallon of tap water takes four hours to process into zero parts per million, pure water. It is easy to clean with a bit of white vinegar. Just use enough to cover the bottom of the machine, let it sit about 5mins., then wipe with a non-abrasive scrubbie. The sides will come clean with a wipe. Rinse out and refill for another round.

After seeing this disgusting mystery crap, there is just no way I can cook stuff in tap water ever again. Running the distiller overnight, every night, is an easy habit that pays-off. The downside is a fan noise and heat generated by the device. The upside is my home retains a lot of the warmth so I wake-up to a cozy kitchen every morning. Summertime was a bit rougher, but so what? It hasn't increased my electricity bill that I can see, and is worth the warming effect.

A gallon of water goes fast, especially if you cook with it. These $10 stackable, 3-gallon water containers, found at Wal-Mart, are super handy.

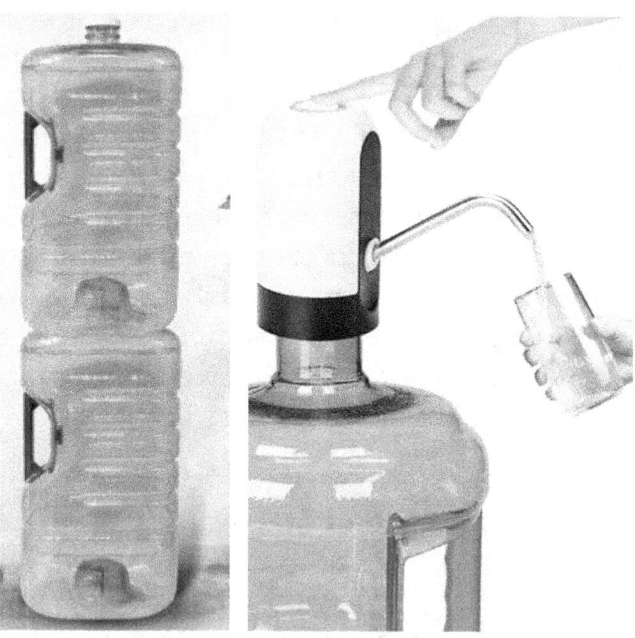

This USB rechargeable water dispenser is under twenty

bucks and an invaluable device for both 3- and 5-gallon water containers.

◆ ◆ ◆

Circumstances rule men; men don't rule circumstances.

Ending up homeless can happen in a flash, and through no fault of your own. Being prepared for most anything will bring you peace of mind if 'most anything' happens.

Three years ago, I never thought this way, ever. Witnessing several fires, various reactions and outcomes, has amounted to wake-up calls in a big way.

And who knew we needed to question the *safety* of our food, or availability of water? Who'd have thunk it necessary to learn about canning food because grocery stores only have three days' worth on-hand, at best? This has always been the case, but *I was asleep at the wheel* and took availability for granted.

Who knew 2k U.S. food processing plants mysteriously burned down in the last 18 months...and aren't coming back? It wasn't on lamestream media, was it? By the way, if you are looking for better news coverage vs scripted talking heads, make it "Redacted." Their YouTube channel is a solid resource for news you can use.

Five years ago, when I moved into my apartment, I had no idea how much pain, loss and expense could be brought on by others. Spinning hay into gold, with an attitude of 'what *can* I do about this?' prompted the Dumbass book, my Dumbass podcast (hehe - i love saying that), and multiple "head's up" chapters in the Rattled Awake Anthology series.

Action takes the edge off anxiety

Are you where I was a few years ago, thinking everything is fine-and-dandy and always will be? Well, my friend, times have changed, and so have people. If you have questions, or want expertise that will save you hours of research, please reach out to me on the OWWLL app. I'm sitting on a lot of information that could benefit you both in terms of inner peace, and preparation.

Don't be scared - you can prepare. You can become a Stormin' Norman, too.

Did this article rattle you awake with at least one aha; one thing you can do, today, to better protect yourself and your family? Please share it with everyone you know and love so they won't get caught barefoot and wearing PJs in public.

Awareness + Acceptance (seeing what IS) + Action = Prepared for most anything

Please leave a review on Amazon, so others can see the value in getting *rattled* enough to act, too.

Lonnee Rey is on a mission to help others who want to better prepare for 'most anything.' Publishing, podcasting, and story development inquiries are some of her favorite topics to gab about, too. Find her on the OWWLL app to speak confidentially about your ideas or aha's. She can fill gaps of information and get you on your way with proven know-how and a passion to share it. Connect with her here: OfficialRattledAwake.com

ARE YOU SURE?...MARIO BEKES

I was taught to be careful what I hoped for, and as a child, despite being warned, I desired hard, because dreams come true, somehow, in the shape, size, or form you least expect.

I wanted to live in a world where everyone is equal, where you don't have to hide your faith or who you're in love with.

That is what I prayed for, and I recall on January 15, 1992, when temperatures dropped below zero and frostbite caused metal to stick together, rendering practically all of our weapons worthless; I also remember my country, Croatia, being internationally recognized on that day.

However, the enemy did not like that and shelled and bombarded our positions and city, making 95% of my troops hide inside a shipping container buried in the ground, where we slept, ate, and cried.

And I remember seeing an advertisement while standing on the door of that container, with my eye on some ancient TV we had.

I told everyone that one day I would be on a plane flying

into a nation where there are McDonalds and girls in bikinis,

What do you think?! Be cautious what you wish for, since on November 18, 1998, I was on my way to Australia, full of chicks and McDonald's!

I was rather sent by the Croatian government to work as a member of Directorate VII - security intelligence services - in the Croatian Embassy in Australia.

Imagine you live in a world where freedom is handed to you by birth, with no constraints and no exceptions. Freedom is guaranteed regardless of skin colour, race, or religion, and that freedom is in a land that has never suffered wars or conquerors, but is rich in all natural resources, iron ore, uranium, cattle, and sheep, and is bordered by oceans.

That country is known as Australia, and it is no surprise that many people consider it to be a dream vacation even today.

Let us fast forward to the year 2020 and Autumn, when all social media platforms, all media sources, and all governments throughout the world become united in the message "we are all going to die from Covid 19" for the first time, and the world comes to a halt.

People stayed at home to work together to eradicate this dreadful sickness, for which everyone was guessing and investigating.

And on the home front in Australia, things began to take the shape of what I saw as a child and teenager, a totalitarian regime disguised under the guise of "we are here to help you!" meaning the government is here to tell you what to do, how to do it, and when to do it, and if you try to say or do something that will upset the government, you are in trouble.

For me, freedom was only a word. Freedom existed only on History Channel documentaries.

During those dreadful times, Hollywood stars rushed to Australia to protect themselves; such a horde of phony heroes, but that was our reality, and these are the same people who preach about freedom.

And, in the midst of that dreadful pandemic, Australia was a safe haven, shielded from virus invasion by oceans.

However, Australia was not immune to serious thought by residents who wondered, "Why are we so limited in our freedoms!?"

Few things frightened me more than the fact that the government publicly asked citizens to spy on each other and report them.

This is the strategy we employed in communist Yugoslavia to create an army of informants, which I believe even the STASI (East German Secret Police) would be proud of.

Needless to say, I couldn't believe how quickly things could escalate in a free country like Australia, and that police could become so brutal, vicious, and vindictive, to the point where I believe they enjoyed shooting people with rubber bullets, breaking old women's and girls' bones, twisting them so they could arrest them for sitting in a park?

That is not freedom; on the contrary, it is something I cannot even articulate, yet it weighs me down to my bones.

Then I reminded myself that Freedom and Democracy come at a cost, therefore let me tell you a story that most people don't see about the ultimate sacrifice for love, freedom.

Imagine living in society where Freedom is given to you by birth, no rules no exceptions. Freedom is guaranteed regardless of what type of skin colour you are, what race, religion and that Freedom is in the country which never experienced wars, conquerors but a country which is so rich with all natural minerals, iron ore, uranium, cattle, sheep, surrounded by oceans.

That country is Australia, even today for many a dream destination.

Now let's fast forward to 2020 and Autumn, it was a time where the only news, the only idea was how to survive a terrible virus and how to protect yourself from it.

Needless to say that during those terrible times, Hollywood stars flew in Australia to protect themselves; such a bunch of fake heroes, but it was our reality.

And in the midst of that deadly pandemic Australia was a safe haven, protected by oceans from virus arrival. However, Australia wasn't protected from deep thinking by citizens whose thoughts were "why are we so limited in our freedoms!?"

Well, little did we know that, for example, the state of Victoria, Australia, and their ferocious leadership would squash any idea of free thinking by arming police to the teeth - sort of paramilitary units I will say, seeing their tactics and how they were handling "Questions of

Freedom."

Then I reminded myself that Freedom and Democracy have a price tag, so let me share a story with you that most people don't see, and that is the ultimate sacrifice for love, freedom.

So frequently, I see and hear about freedom, democracy, and free speech mixed up in continuous social media posts about conspiracy theories.

But I'd like to tell you a true story of how expensive and violent the true cost of freedom can be.

To begin, I'd like to clarify that I was not born in a so-called free society where people could freely express themselves; this was not the case.

On the contrary, I was born in a completely different society: communism. I didn't know anything better except that every now and then someone would come from the West and bring some magazines. My crew was more interested in porn magazines, while the girls were more interested in music-related magazines. Ah well, we loved women from the West, girls, and male musicians from the West.

Growing up wasn't difficult because I, too, desired things from the West, such as Nike sneakers or Levi's trousers. I was living a life of daydreaming, with the occasional slap from my father telling me to stop dreaming that "one day I will do this or that" and that my destiny is sealed: "I will be factory worker and, on my tombstone, will be written born and died in same city, saw nothing, no legacy except debts."

I didn't want it, and I often tell people to be careful what they hope for because dreams do come true.

I wanted to be a Rambo, a Chuck Norris one-man army, a Swiss knife, but I also wanted to be a professional soldier, an officer in special forces...and my aspirations were accomplished.

I was 18 years old when military police officials from the Yugoslav People's Army knocked on my door on July 14, 1991.

I had been drinking since the previous day because the lady who had been my life's love had suddenly become my "enemy" overnight. Why? Because she and her parents were Serbians and Orthodox, I, Croatian and Roman Catholic, and in less than 24 hours we shall be at war with each other.

So that morning, I heard a loud slamming on my door. I was exhausted from being drunk all day and night, and even before I opened it, they instructed me to go to the army barracks because the country needed me.

For the time being, I was perplexed as to who needed me, what country needed me, and what conflict needed me. As Yugoslavia disintegrated, Croatia declared independence.

At that point, I had to decide whether I wanted to fight for communist Yugoslavia or for my own country, where freedom of speech is guaranteed, there is no fear of secret police, we can have heaps of McDonalds, porn magazines, and Coke, all because that was the definition of democracy for many of us... until the first bombardment by the Yugoslav People's Army.

In less than 24 hours, I witnessed utter damage, death, the

odour of burning corpses, demolished buildings, and cars.

On another point, I have nowhere else to go. I discovered a note written by my parents that they left on the kitchen table the night before, saying "We are OK." Those were my parents' final words.

So, my Alpha Male father has fled? No way. But he did, as did many other alpha men. Average Joes, like myself, stayed to fight this new war, a war for freedom without comprehending the true cost of freedom.

After finishing my first training for special forces for the Ministry of Interior in seven days, I was transported into the pinnacle battalion. It consisted of ex-convicts, figures from the criminal world, and the list goes on, but I must say they were the tip of the spear in every single event I could recall.

You can learn by watching, reading, or participating in all of the above, because war is harsh in all shapes, sizes, and forms.

I can't tell you how many methods humans devised to take lives, murder people, and save people, but war isn't about dating or being happy; it's about turning ordinary men into machines.

In my head, I tried not to become one of those machines, but the conflict didn't stop. Day after day, night after night, there was close and constant combat.

Summer 1991 was beautiful and warm and sunny, unlike past summers. I'd been in the war for just over two months.

The following experience occurred in that summer of

1991, in a village in East Slavonia, Croatia. This was where I witnessed for the first time what war does to people, how war changes lives, and how costly the price of freedom is:

We returned to the large, white home. A beautiful 2-story, it was the spot chosen for us to recuperate and relax. It also appeared to be an ideal target for the enemy, but it was the only house that had not been shot at.

Something deep inside me told me that this house wouldn't last much longer. It wasn't until later that we discovered it was being used as a marker, or lighthouse, as it was easily visible to enemy forces. Once combat commenced, no doubt they would use that house as orientation where to shoot. In that way, they were able to line up ammunition against us and would certainly destroy the house by shelling it.

I went upstairs to a spotless bedroom with a king-sized bed, white linens, and cushions. I couldn't believe how spotless it was. Even the bedding smelled fresh, as if they had been washed just a few days before. The window was open, and the curtains were dancing in it. You'd think there was nothing out of the ordinary going on in the house.

I sat on the edge of the bed, wondering if it was OK to lie down and soil the clean covers with my soiled outfit.

On the bedside table was a photograph of a husband and wife. There was a closet facing the bed. The photograph next to it depicted the couple with their two daughters. I remember thinking there was a significant age gap between the girls.

Where had these individuals gone? I pondered. Did they realise we were in their house, fighting an army?

My assistant then entered and offered me a cup of coffee. We talked briefly before I told him I needed to crash and requested he come fetch me in ten minutes.

I glanced in the mirror at myself, all covered in black dust, then lay down and fell asleep. I fantasized about making love; it was so lovely. A few rounds ricocheted off the house, startling me awake.

I perched on the edge of the bed and drank the coffee, trying to come to my senses, trying to be brave. "You know why you're here," I assured myself. Take charge. You've got this."

I looked down and, to my surprise, discovered a book from basic school. Their daughter must have brought it here to show her folks. It brought a smile to my face.

They must have fled quickly, I thought.

I began reading the stories and notes the girl had scribbled in the book's margins, and the memories returned to me.

I saw a lot of blank pages at the end of the book. Because of the war, school must have been cancelled, and nothing was written in May and June.

"My father is a police officer," she wrote on the last page. "My mother claims she can no longer live this way. She is heartbroken. My father does not want to leave."

Ah, so it was the residence of a communist-era police official. I placed the book next to my coffee cup.

I decided to open the wardrobe carefully because it was

ajar. The front door squeaked. Inside, the husband and wife were hanging out.

I inhaled deeply. I grabbed a blanket, threw it down on the floor, and covered them up before searching the other rooms for the girls. I discovered their nearly vacant chambers. There were not many clothes or books.

They must have left and the parents returned for whatever reason. Perhaps they didn't want to leave their home? Maybe our arrival trapped them in the closet? I'm not sure.

For this miserable couple, 'until death do us part' was literally true.

I kept fighting in the war for the following 4.5 years, and it was one of the most cruel and horrific experiences of my life.

Finally, I'd like you to consider what happened in the last five years that jolted you awake.

My first impression was that you were writing about Australian issues, freedom, and the illusion of freedom.

I've been in this great country for 25 years and there hasn't been a day when I haven't told myself how fortunate I am to live here.

What I couldn't understand and still don't understand is how quickly people relinquish their ideals, lifestyles, and desire to be free and equal, literally overnight.

Then I remember as a kid hearing stories of how valiant resistance fighters in WWII were, especially partisans against Germans, and now this?

We are giving away freedom so easily just to be told what we must do, how and in what way - okay, I can buy into that, rules and laws exist for a reason - but what I can't understand and will never understand is that freedom of speech has been squashed and openly displayed by the government what can happen to you if you decide to say "opposite."

Then I take a deep breath and apply reasoning. Of course, it is simple to give up "freedoms" handed to you by birth because you, them, have never fought for freedom and have made no sacrifices to retain that freedom.

Freedom does not come cheap; it is the product of collective or individual sacrifice for what is right.

Mario Bekes is on a mission to elevate minds and highlight brilliant people with life-changing stories. His YouTube channel has over 100 videos on personal growth, exploring criminal behaviour, true crime and tips for making the most of your life. He is the *Guinness World Records Holder 2023* in continuous audio broadcasting, an Ambassador and Activist for Humanity, served 1,800 consecutive combat days in WAR against communism, tyranny for democracy and freedom, and Ex-Military security intelligence, & Diplomatic security intelligence - Republic of Croatia. Connect with him here: **https://www.mariobekes.com.au/**

CRACKS IN THE FOUNDATION… CHEF SHAWN MONROE

Hindsight Is 2020

Dedicated to my family:

And all families who struggle with life balance, work and mental exhaustion.

Introduction

They say we are drawn to the ocean and for many reasons and for me personally, I come to breathe and be inspired by the awesomeness. The sounds, smells and the constant pounding of the waves reminds me nothing is permanent. Like in nature, things are evolving and the ebb and flow of how physics, chemistry and biology all work harmoniously is magical. The first time I saw the ocean I was 12 years old. My sister's boyfriend at the time wanted to take me to Daytona, Florida and Disney World. My mother was nervous but finally said yes, knowing that she would never be able to afford it, or have the time to take me. The main reason why she was nervous was because my sister's boyfriend wanted to take me on this Florida road trip on his motorcycle. I would be riding on the back, 1200 miles one way, stopping every time it rained, hanging out under a bridge until the rain passed. We stayed at a hotel three times during the trip to be safe and to explore other things along the way, like south of the border. This experience set in motion a path I would embrace my whole life: to cherish experiences over possessions. After I read *The Old Man and the Sea*, my love and respect for the ocean and Ernest Hemingway's writing/adventures blossomed and, in the years, to come I would travel to all the places he was known to go:

The Ritz Paris and Hemingways Bar https://www.ritzparis.com/

Harrys Bar in NYC, Paris and Venice https://www.harrysbar.com/

La Venencia for house made Sherry's http://www.lavenencia.com/

Lhardy for croqueta and veal en croute https://lhardy.com/

The Palace Hotel for cocktails https://www.marriott.com/en-us/hotels/madwi-the-westin-palace-madrid/overview/?scid=f2ae0541-1279-4f24-b197-a979c79310b0

Cerveceria Alemana for beer and Iberico pork https://www.cerveceriaalemana.com/main/

Bar Marsella for house made vermouth in Barcelona, Spain.

Years later, after working a long and crazy busy season

at my restaurant, I was able to go back to Florida and visit Hemingway's home in Key West. I enjoyed all the excitement, food and even went deep sea fishing and caught a sailfish! What a rush to bring in a trophy fish that big and powerful, then take a picture before releasing back into the ocean.

Hemingway's favorite hangout in Key West was Sloppy Joes, walking distance to his home, of course.

https://www.hemingwayhome.com

https://sloppyjoes.com/

In the next 20 years, my wife, Angela, and I, have made it our mission to travel to all the places, bars and restaurants where Hemingway was known to go. We are inspired by both the want, and the need, to travel; seeking adventures in our lives. These are a few places that we visited so far in our travels: Idaho, Kansas City. New York City, Italy, France and just recently, Spain. We went to the oldest restaurant in the world and a Hemingway hangout! Called Botin, we had the tableside suckling pig and it was amazing! Sidenote: their wood fire oven has never gone out...since 1725. https://botin.es/en/home/

Someday, we will go to Cuba and Africa, where he spent a lot of time. My fascination with Ernest Hemingway began as most, with his readings, but became more involved when finding out this great literary struggled with work and mental exhaustion. I needed to know more about how this man could be so great but yet flawed and human. Visiting locations he frequented allowed me have a glimpse into the places that gave him respite and escape.

At 57, I have worked in several states in the USA, mainly New York, Florida, Wisconsin and Texas. I presently live in San Antonio, TX, and Indian Rocks, FL. This is my culinary journey of food, wine, events and private jet catering experience, yes, but more about how, in this fast-paced exciting business your focus can be so extreme you lose some of your self and family structure. This is a story of how I got myself back to a place of happiness with my family, and got my life back on track. When you are working at this pace, letting go of all the huge responsibilities is harder than you might think.

When you're an Executive Chef in Michelin- and Mobile-starred restaurants, you are in a symphony of talented chefs, sommeliers and servers. The Executive Chef is the conductor, picking out all the notes, modes and flavors in season to entertain and excite the palate of the guests and gourmands. Like most chefs in the world, we tend to put a lot of passion, love and art in our craft to the point we don't see how much our careers flatline relationships. Our wives, husbands, children and family all take a back seat in this amazing, exciting but all-consuming business that we love.

We take foundations for granted, that they will always hold, always be strong. But they do crack and buckle. When we take care of our foundation, we can build a tower worth our families and career legacy.

One of the first cracks in my foundation was when I was Executive Chef at a four-star, Pierce's 1894 Restaurant in Elmira NY. I was 27 and I lived in Ithaca NY, traveling back and forth the 40-minute one way drive. I was working 12 hours plus, six days a week. This equates to being away every weekend, holiday and lots of missed special occasions in your family's day to day. When you love what you do so much and the focused energy, dedication and discipline to be the best, to lead a team that has the same drive, often we lose sight of other very important things. Namely, our health, families, hobbies and quality sleep. After eight months working and living at this pace, my wife looked at me and said "Wow you have lost a lot of weight." I laughed it off but soon jumped on the scale; I had lost 20 lbs. I remember thinking I never really gave myself time to eat and with my job, tasting food is constant; fine tuning recipes, rich sauces and the timeline stress was always on. The excitement of being an executive chef at a prestigious 100-year-old restaurant was my life, and I knew it would be a great restaurant to fine tune my cuisine. I did my first "Barrel dinner," which is a tasting of the best of the (wine harvest) Finger Lakes wines paired with a menu I created. My staff and I worked tirelessly for three days leading up to the event, sourcing-out the best products locally and all over the world. Timing all this together with the wineries, sommeliers and owners, meanwhile keeping the regular business going and preparing for a Barrel dinner, this was exciting and exhilarating. I had weeks like this all the time because Pierce's 1894 restaurant was a destination where guests would come in from NYC and the surrounding area.

One night I left the restaurant...it was a very cold night, with light rain and temperatures down in the 20s. I was driving back home, got on the highway on-ramp and hit black ice (ice sitting on top of the road that you can't see.) I started fishtailing and was careful not to hit the brakes, but my truck spun uncontrollably and hit the shoulder of the road. I started tumbling over and over, rolling the truck three or four times until it stopped. All I could hear was

"Welcome to the Jungle " by Guns and Roses playing on the car radio and the engine hissing. I unbuckled my seatbelt and jumped out of my truck through all the shattered glass everywhere. I had to look myself over to make sure I didn't have any injuries. Thankfully, I had put on my seatbelt because it saved my life. By some miracle, I made it through without serious injuries. I was happy to be alive and with only having some back issues and a really bad headache, I just wanted to hug my family and feel blessed. Later, the constant nightmares and flashbacks to the accident put me in major depression and anxiety. I remember having this sensation that would come over me, as if someone cracked an egg on my head and the yolk would slowly drip down over my whole body. I would try to fall asleep whenever I could, as a way to disconnect from this frequent sensation. Even in my chef's office I would sleep before getting into my truck for the long ride home, just to ease anxiety of making the long drive. Getting back in a vehicle was hard but I needed to go back to work. That loss of confidence driving in the new truck was unnerving. This life changing accident would alter my priorities for the next few years. In fact, I ended up leaving that job right about the time my son was born. I was still shaken to the core that I was in a near-death accident where my wife Angela, daughter Chelsey and son Taylor would be left without me.

As a child I grew up with eight brothers and sisters. We had rough times then. My parents' divorce, poverty and economic times of the 70s and early 80s made for a challenging youth. The earliest times I remember started in the kitchen was just eight years old. My brother and I would be hungry, head into the kitchen, and play a game we called "let's go invent." We looked through cupboards, the refrigerator and freezer to see what we could come up with.

There was not much food, but when you're hungry you figure it out and get creative. At first, we started with easy things that we assumed were easy to make like making box mac n cheese, reading and following simple recipes, adding things like bacon or canned tuna to make it more interesting. Often there were missing ingredients like milk and butter but we could improvise with other ingredients such as powdered or evaporated milk and macaroni water. This always made the finished product "interesting." Later, I started tinkering with ideas, some good and some terrible. This early forming exercise of survival led me to cook several different snacks and treats for my brother and sister. I just know they will read this and say, "You made us make you cinnamon toast and then you would yell 'out!' *but don't touch it with your grubby fingers*." This was a fun time with my siblings, was the beginning of my culinary journey and the thrill of feeding people.

We always had lots of potatoes so I would set up a pan of oil, make fried potatoes and serve with ketchup or mayonnaise. I love the skin on fried potatoes and still don't understand why people are so wasteful with their food by peeling them. I had to be careful not to burn myself in this process. Hindsight being 2020, it scares me to think of one of my own children hovering over a hot stove frying potato. I did it and I learned early about the temperature and how to adjust the flames on a stove, draining excess fat off and salting while they were still hot.

Living during this time was tough, fighting hunger and being alone in the house for long periods of time while my single mother worked. I remember being told I was the man of the house back then. Seems like a lot to put on a young boy but I guess I needed to grow up faster than others. We loved each other and always stuck it through. With all the cracks in our foundation there was still a solid base we could build from.

My first real chef job was for the Panache sky bar in the Ithaca Hotel, but was called the Ramada Inn Tower then. I made all the appetizers and salads for anyone that wanted anything while enjoying the view and drinks. I had some direction, but they soon let me "invent" some of my own appetizers. I was 18 then. The more I learned the more my passion grew along with the ability to handle larger responsibilities. Getting used to the long hours over cutting boards, stoves and excessive temperatures, standing on my feet for 12 hours plus, got easier with time. When I was a chef's apprentice at the Ithaca Country Club, I learned all the menu and recipes for making sauces and soups in a fast-paced kitchen environment with multiple events, 200 seat restaurant and poolside grill, etc. Like many of us in the kitchen, we are always looking to learn and be current in the food world. When opportunities present themselves, like they did when an Executive Chef would leave abruptly or would be fired, you must jump at the chance to prove yourself worthy of this next level. While working in this new position I would spend hours in the library and purchase cookbooks of all the chefs that I admired. Working and studying the craft was a time consuming mission and one that took complete focus. The long hours didn't permit a lot of extra time; it was then I incorporated the saying "there is time for sleep when I'm dead." This crack in the foundation seemed like it was a reasonable one to look past. Years later I would understand the true value of good sleep.

These great Chef's were my go-to for inspiration and knowledge:

Escoffier, Robuchon, Bocuse; I learned all the classic French and popular dishes, soups and sauce techniques, which ignited my passion and respect for cultural cuisines. I would research, cook, taste and adjust flavors as well as reading and learning about the lifestyles and the people who created it. I would go to specialty shops and farmers markets to source out different products in season and items I wanted to experiment with. Every week I would explore different regional recipes like Mexican, New Orleans, Caribbean, and South American foods. Later I got into Asian, Mediterranean and Eastern European.

Like many other chefs, we learn from our mothers, fathers and grandparents with them sharing traditions over holiday meals and gatherings. Later as we grow, we inspire new traditions but often with adaptations that have been passed down. My mother was a huge influence in the kitchen. She grew up in Ithaca, NY, and we were fortunate it was a small college town with plenty of diversity. My mother would experiment with Mediterranean foods and healthy ingredients like tofu, carib, falafel, granola, etc. Often, we would end up with tofu in lasagna which isn't embraced by many children. As an adult I now recognize not only her efforts to provide healthy food for her family but also the creativity she was using to expand our young palates.

I went on to be Executive Chef at Pierce's 1894 four-star/four- diamond Dirona awarded restaurant.

Coyote Loco Restaurant and Cantina

Banfis - Statler Hotel School at Cornell University teaching and training Cornell students to run a full-scale restaurant. There, I worked with the Guest Chef series. This was a series that let students work with famous visiting chefs and was under the direction of Giuseppe Pezzotti, Senior Lecturer and my life mentor. I was fortunate to be a chosen chef to participate in this series. We received all the recipes and instructions from the celebrity chefs and worked the whole week with them shoulder to shoulder. Cooking with the great chefs visiting Cornell University took a lot of coordination leading up to the week of the dinner. Student managers were picked by skill levels and their ability to handle this responsibility for a Michelin experience. My student sous chefs: Michael Dean, Jehrome Thigpen and David Samuels were in that role. Keep in mind these students were going to school full time and working at a busy restaurant. Their devotion to their education and career path gave me inspiration to want to continue pushing my personal boundaries. After all, exhaustion was just one more crack....right?

The guest chefs included Chef Wolfgang Puck, (33yo me with Puck, right); Chef Emeril Lagasse, (below)

Chef Daniel Boloud and Chef Mashahara Morimoto, to name a few. This was one of the best five years of my life and I felt privileged to work alongside these amazing chefs. After the last course went out we all had a "family dinner" which is the entire restaurant, kitchen staff, management, teachers and the celebrity chefs all eating together talking about how things went, followed by Q&A with the chef.

We always had an after-hours get together to get to know each other, have a great glass of wine, and be in the moment. This helped as a debriefing and a much-needed time to breathe and laugh. During these after-hours I could reflect on the reason I loved the craft and the coworkers. It was the reason to get up and do it all again. Too much thought beyond those moments seemed like time that could be wasted. I left Cornell in 2001, as I felt inspired to get back into the excitement of the restaurant world. It was bittersweet to leave the academic environment but I knew these great memories were forever. I have many culinary brothers and sisters all over the world, running their own business and restaurants, all of which makes me smile.

From Cornell I went to :

Executive Chef at Maders Restaurant-

Creator of Best Care Cuisine / Science of Food at 30,000 for Midwest Airlines, Milwaukee and Kansas City.

I partnered and owned the fourth largest Private Jet Catering Service in the USA, as well as Creative Catering Solutions in Texas, Creative Catering Solutions, Catering by Chef Shawn

{These are two of our in-flight meals}

I am a preferred catering chef for The Alamo -UNESCO World Heritage Site. The Alamo in San Antonio, TX.

My companies do themed private events for 10 to 4000 people in multiple cities. I even catered the Super Bowl! You might remember that game: it was the Super Bowl that Tom Brady and the New England Patriots came back from halftime down 03 to 28 Atlanta Falcons and won 34 to 28 upset!

I have fed countless celebrities, rockstars, politicians and executives all over the world. I will never look back and feel like I didn't do enough or see enough. In my 30 plus years as Executive Chef/Entrepreneur I have had times where the responsibility and excessive hours would put a major strain on my family and myself. I have worked 90 plus hours a week and at times for 8 to10 weeks without days off. When starting Best Care Cuisine for Midwest Airlines I researched and studied the science of food at 30,000 ft. Taking many foods and products up on a 737 aircraft with just a few Midwest Airlines executives, myself and my Sous Chef, Andrew Monk. Chef Andrew Monk has worked alongside me in many kitchens throughout the USA and was a force and dear friend I could always count on. We were cooking, tasting and researching how and why we lose 20% of our taste due to cabin pressure, altitude and dry air. I created all the recipes and menus to compensate for the loss of taste we endure while flying but also to be careful with salts and saturated fats due to a condition called deep vein thrombosis, which can occur in inflight. This is when we are sitting in cramped places for long periods of time in an airplane cabin. We were making 3000 meals a day in Milwaukee and Kansas City. I was also running Maders Restaurant and our catering division with NASCAR Formula One and Grand Prix Miller Brewing Company, Harley Davidson, Summer Fest, and Pabst Theatre. I had several head chefs, sous chefs and 100s of employees to get all this done but nonetheless, it all came at a big cost with burn out/ mental exhaustion.

I attempted to use playing an instrument as a way of

destressing and getting feelings out. Playing guitar and writing my own songs began at age 14, now I was hoping it could be more than amusement and add some much-needed downtime to my life. This expression of making music and writing songs, thoughts and poetry has been a major lifeline in my wellbeing. The vibration of a guitar next to my body and releasing soulful feelings, started to quiet my busy mind.

When I finally got all the systems going well within the restaurant, I would retreat to the escape of my bed. For days, I would remotely stay tethered to my cell phone handling day-to-day issues. This was another time when I saw cracks, but as most humans do, we think "just keep going and it will get better."

It was Christmas time and I was off early on a Sunday. Me and my family planned a fun evening to watch *It's A Wonderful Life,* and make homemade pizza together. I felt very emotional during the scene when George Bailey was sitting in Martinis Bar after finding out Uncle Billy lost $8,000 (that's $170,000 in 2023) and the auditor had a warrant for his arrest. Scattered and worried about going to jail and all of his missed opportunities in life he folded his hands and prayed. "God, God dear Heavenly Father in Heaven, I am not a praying man, if you're up there and you can hear me, show me the way. I'm at the end of my rope. Show me the way, God." I had my children, Chelsey and Taylor on either side of me and a tear ran down my face. Something cracked inside releasing that tear. I connected to this character's pain in trying to be everything he needed to be as a husband, father and the thought of letting anyone down. I felt the tight choked-up feeling building in the back of my throat and quickly composed myself, as to not let any crack appear; instead, just snuggling deeper into the arms of my children. The scene continues and Clarence the guardian angel comes to save the day and show George how much he has meant to everyone in his family, friends and his community. Going through scene after scene, where George gets his wish: that it would have been better if he was never born at all. He runs to the bridge where he saved Clarence from drowning and folds his hands again praying saying, "Clarence get me back, get me back to my wife and kids!" my emotions just burst and I had to leave the family room! As I was welling up and attempting to take deep breaths, I kept hearing the little girl in *It's a Wonderful Life*, saying 'what's wrong with daddy' and the son saying 'should we pray for daddy.' With my wife and kids looking worried, and me feeling cracked and broken due to mental exhaustion, I had to go outside in the cold and breathe in and out. I knew what I was feeling was not normal and questioned if this is what a breakdown was. All I wanted was time with my wife and kids/quality family time. I had never had these kinds of moments before.

It wasn't long after that I made different arrangements with my staff and schedules to try to cover the crack that had formed and hoped this change would help everything. My identity was in turmoil. Even coming home to my family sometimes felt like I was a stranger, not being part of their everyday existence, having to catch up. Not knowing what was going on in my family's life and various household issues was difficult for all. Moving forward, Angela and I had to make different arrangements to keep our family together by doing midnight snacks with daddy on Friday and Saturday nights, and enjoying 'Sunday Funday' if I had the day off. My family matters so much and after all we have been through to keep a strong and stable unit - this was the foundation that had to stay solid even if the ground was shifting.

Moving my family from their hometown twice in their young life was tough but the opportunity to make a lot more money and growth for me as a chef partner made sense at the time. Again, my family rallied to encourage my career and we knew with each opportunity the challenge would be there but were hopeful that contentment and peace of mind would exist also. Blissful expectations.

Whitefish Bay, Wisconsin, was where we bought our first family home. With all my work hours and running multiple businesses, Milwaukee, Kansas City, (Chicago for seasonal business), I wanted my family in a safe place with the best school district we could afford. As the years went on I missed a lot of special occasions in my children's lives. Angela would take care of everything in regard to the house, our children, Chelsey and Taylor, and all their activities, homework and the normal day-to-day stuff. It got to the point that I was missing my family so much I would leave work and come back when I could. We asked our children to pick what recital or sports event, etc., they wanted me to be at, as chances were I might only be able to attend one or two from the many. I made sure that I was at this one event for each of them. One occasion was when my daughter Chelsey was having a flute solo in her school band concert and I raced to the school from my work to see her perform. I waved to her and she gave a little wave back to show she saw me and the little smile she gave me meant the world. Jumping back into the car to drive back to the restaurant knowing I kept my promise, sometimes that is all I had. I ran into my son Taylor's wrestling match, keeping that promise but wasn't able to hug him after his win, with the same *must get back to work* issue. Later, we would go to a restaurant and celebrate. These are my wonderful children and they make me a better man. It is now that I realize filling the cracks with love can reinforce our foundations.

No one will ever see the small cracks or problems in your life until your foundation is shaken. Small cracks become weak and over time any strong structures without care and reinforcement will succumb to this misfortune.

In 2020, the foundation for millions of us was shaken! The blame, worry and confusion of what will happen next, or, can we even fix our foundations, seemed bleak. There was unsettling fake news misreporting, and bad science clouding our judgment; hearing the number of deaths perpetuated this "fear movement."

Like many other families we had emergency meetings and phone calls trying to get our kids home safe from college/ other cities so we could all be together and stay safe. My wife Angela was amazing and like a family hero getting all the kids home. She was adamant that she be the only one to go to get supplies and meticulously sanitize all the products coming into the house. At times I remember looking at this as a war against the American way of life, and wondered who was behind this?

The first to get Covid 19 was my son Taylor and his fiancé Dria, coming back from the 'NYC war scene,' with the massive deaths they reported every day. We finally got them back and quarantined them in one room, and had a system of getting food supplies etc. to them every day for 10 days till we felt everything was safe. Our daughter, who was in Austin, TX, traveled to San Antonio to be safe with us. As we watched all this unfold, a lot of people thought (like we did) "this can't be happening." Not in America!! Pegged to the news and getting misinformation was a huge crack in our country's foundation. They say, "hindsight is 2020" and is in the history of pandemics and epidemics of our past.

In 1918, over 100 years ago, the world had a pandemic, for example; humans are not immune to the ideas of sickness, disease epidemics and pandemics. We have learned this throughout the millennium, to be ready, to be prepared. Just not the world all at once - in the modern times of fast travel from every country and even faster communications through the internet, social media and TV.

My whole family got Covid throughout this time, all at different times (God Bless) and we all got through it.

Before the Pandemic, I sold my private jet catering companies/events and we began to travel all over the world on food, wine and cultural explorations. My wife and I enjoy exploring new places, having what she calls "happy accidents" when we get lost and find amazing nuggets throughout our travels. This has been our life's journey and passion. To go, to learn and find new ideas in culture (people/music), food, wine, architecture and landscape.

My family means a great deal to me and this unprecedented time in history opened up our minds and hearts to our human frailty.

When we finally got everyone safe home and better, I started thinking about how this two-month quarantine (stay home rule) was going to affect our mental space and boredom. We set up several quiet spaces in our home, opened the backyard pool and sitting areas to get sun, breathe, and try to get away from the news. As a chef/entrepreneur and event planner, I started thinking maybe we need to make our home into themed menu nights with food/drinks, with movies that correlate with the theme.

Italian Night

Prosecco and Chicken piccata, Chianti and pasta pappardelle with Bolognese.

Music for the day: Pavarotti, Andrea Bocelli, Frank Sinatra, Maria Callas and Micheal Bublé

Movies for the day: The Godfather, Moon Struck, Il Postino, Good Fellas, Mystic Pizza

<u>Chicken Piccata</u>

1 c Seasoned flour

1/3 c Egg wash

4-2 to 3 oz Chicken scallopini (pounded thin)

2 tbsp Olive oil

1 large Garlic Clove

1 tbsp Shallots

2/3 c Chicken stock

1!4 c white wine

2 tbsp Capers

2 Tbsp chopped. Italian parsley.

1/2 to 1 Lemon juice. Zest 1/2 tsp

To taste Salt and pepper

2 tbsp Butter or olive oil to finish sauce.

Slice chicken into scallopini and dredge into seasoned flour then into egg wash and back into the seasoned flour. (One dry hand, one wet hand); set aside

Fine dice shallots and garlic.

Rough chop parsley

In sauté pan heat and coat pan with olive oil on med high heat. Add seasoned flour chicken cutlets 3 to 5 min., turn chicken, sauté for additional 3 to 5 min., and add shallots, garlic, capers and additional olive oil. 2 to 3 min Add white wine, chicken stock and lemon juice. Adjust sauce with salt pepper and olive oil or butter.

Mexican Night

Margarita with Carnitas served with toasted tortilla cilantro and lime, Salsa Verde

Modelo beer with Ancho chili chicken quesadilla with jalapeño cilantro crema

Mexican rice

Borracha beans

Music for the day: Marc Anthony, Enrique Iglesias, Selena, Texas chili peppers

Movies for the day: Like Water for Chocolate, La Bamba, Cocoa, Selena, The Alamo

Carnitas with Salsa Verde

3 lb Pork butt

2 med Onions

6 Garlic cloves

3 Jalapeños

2 lb Tomatillos

2to3 Lime juice and zest.

1 Orange juice and zest

¼ c chopped Cilantro

1 tsp Cumin

2 tsp Chipotle powder

.5 tbsp Onion powder

.5 tsp Garlic granulated.

1 tsp Mexican oregano

2 Bay leaf

.25 cup Oil

Toasted corn and flour tortillas

Crumble queso fresco

Coat pork butt with oil salt and pepper and sear in a large pan that can be covered and placed into the oven with enough water or chicken stock halfway. Cook for 2 hours and add large, chopped onions, garlic, tomatillo, spices, lime juice, zest and oranges. Cook for 2 more hours or until meat pulls apart with ease. Remove meat, limes and oranges and puree to salsa, add cilantro and adjust with oil.

When the pork cools slightly pull apart and remove excessive fat.

In a large skillet, heat the pan with oil and fry pork for 3 to 5 minutes on high. Season with salt and pepper

To serve:

Toasted tortillas

Pork carnitas

Sliced red onion

Cilantro

Salsa verde

Queso Fresca

Crema, optional

We went on to plan several events throughout the pandemic - Chinese, Miami/Cuba, Comfort/Americana, New Orleans. We had lots of fun learning more about cultures and exploring each day with great conversations, outside pool and fireside chat time.

My beautiful wife and I have been together for 41 years on this great American road by reconnecting as a family, finding little cracks and reinforcing our family structure through this very trying time in history. We have worked together on a family wine project, real estate company and a new family business called Creative Catering Solutions, where we collectively share in the joys of planning special events for our customers all over.

My life lesson is this: Check your foundation, look for cracks, but realize we are all human and we have faults. We make mistakes, we say mean things for some of us, we say nothing at all, which can be worse. Reinforce your foundations! Fill in the cracks as they show and protect your human investment in your families. Let us all embrace our foundations and share our stories.

Chef Shawn Monroe is on a mission to show that the balance between our career goals, expectations we place on ourselves, combined with family and life needs, can cause our foundational structure to start cracking. Mental health and relationships can suffer while trying to keep all these plates in the air. The foundation is our personal wellbeing. The balancing act of being a professional, father, husband and human, while having it all, requires recognizing little cracks before they become a foundational issue. He hopes his story will help others recognize the need to take a step back, breathe and handle the small cracks now, while they are still easy to repair. Connect with him here: http://linkedin.com/in/chefshawnmonroe

Chef Monroe is always so dedicated and passionate in the 30 plus years in hospitality. It can be seen when talking to him and his actions. He cares about the guests and the staff that works with him. This is his story in his most honest words. Chef Monroe and I worked together with the Guest Chefs Class at Cornell University Statler Hotel School.
Co-author Chef Shawn /Rattled Awake Vol 5 is inspiring and thought provoking. Highly recommended.

Senior lecturer, Giuseppe Pezzotti
79' Cornell University Statler Hotel School.

There is a lot to be learned by reading Co-author/chef Shawn Monroe in Rattled Awake Vol 5. He writes and shares his true-life journey in the hospitality world.

My wife and I met Chef Shawn when he was Executive Chef at Pierce's 1894 Restaurant in Elmira. When Chef Shawn took over my restaurant, he helped to take our kitchen to a higher level and made a permanent mark on the culinary landscape of Ithaca. I was pleased to know that Chef Shawn went on to my alma mater and the best hospitality school on the planet - Cornell University Statler Hotel School. His culinary journey is one of learning he shares in this series.

John Alexander
CEO Founder of The CBORD Group and former owner of Coyote Loco Restaurant.

NO REGRETS...
MICHELLE LAAKS

What are we going to both do about the adoption thing? I said.

Two weeks ago, a friend text messaged me after our last discussion fifteen years ago. "Shall we get together and catch up?"

She was asking me, "What have I been doing in my life after all this time?" and "What have I done about my adoption story since?"

After all the years of searching for, and finally finding her daughter, all she has is "I don't want to know you." What a shame!

She had given her child up for adoption at birth and always wondered. She was stuck in an ongoing cycle without closure; a fruitless journey that never reached its destination. I always thought about how she must feel being on the other side of my adoption situation. In one way, I knew how she felt, stuck in nowhere land with all these feelings; never knowing nor meeting her daughter must be an instant living nightmare without closure and rebirth of cycles of despair. I always felt for her, as it must be the worst feeling to leave someone being stuck emotionally.

We could have spoken for hours on end, going through something that stopped both our lives in "stuck – mode cycles" really speaks to my heart. Finally getting to speak with someone who understood me is the greatest feeling, ever.

People like her have inspired me to make this my mission and passion to make this come to full cycle. *Here's how I handled adoption*, and here is what I decided to do since the dust settled:

I want to help the person who has not had the opportunity to meet, greet and bond since an adoption took place in their lives. There is still so much left to say. I know from personal experience they have got to get it out anyway! Don't just leave it, don't be stuck! People need to start actioning all this stuff they are carrying.

The ones that have met need to get it out in writing, like I did. Writing makes it real. It gets those thoughts out of your head and onto paper where you can see, feel and deal with it all much better. This is really about the process of expressing deeply-felt emotions. Write it for yourself, first. Get it out and know that's enough!

Write everything that matters to you about your process, "don't carry it" or you will carry it internally and project it outwardly to others until you do! You will discover what your message is and start with your healing. You will have no-regrets by writing and sharing your story, but you might if you don't do it.

It's very necessary, as you go through a transformational and emotional process, because these feelings must get out! I know how it feels. I also know how getting that story published, and the legacy it creates, completes the cycle. I discovered this only twenty four years later, but now I know…now I can help others along my journey.

My passion is to inspire others to have "no regrets" and show them how much growth can, and will, happen in the process.

This is what happened to me: I was going on 30 years old at the time, when my one cousin decided that it was time I knew. Knew what? A secret had been kept from me my whole life; one everyone knew but me. This feels like a cruel joke right?

Finding out I'm adopted late in life destroyed parts of my identity; it turned life upside down. Everyone in my family knew my secret and honoured my mom and dad's wishes, never to tell me. I did not grow up with a stigma, and was so very protected and loved.

As soon as I found out, I was stuck for three years trying to find my family. I could not rest nor let it go, my world stopped in an instant, this seeking and never knowing literally "ate *me alive.*"

Every single minute of every day, staring at the ceiling and thinking about "how they must be feeling," what they look like, what my medical history must be, I've got to find this, this is like a blueprint, written in concrete. This became my journey.

How do I fit into the family tree, do I have siblings, how will they react when they hear from me? Oh, my word, all these questions! Not knowing the truth drove me mad. I had to have closure.

My biological parents must have been wondering how I must be after all this time, that was all I could think of every waking minute.

I was on a mission to find them and thank them for what must have been the hardest decision to make in life to let me go. I knew in my heart that by finding them and connecting with them that it would help us all heal in a big way; that we all would have no regrets.

This always made me wonder why my biological mother took 10 months before letting me go to my adoptive parents. Finding her finally helped me realize how important it was that I could start filling in all the blanks in my life and get out of "I wonder" and back to reality. Being so blessed by my parents I had to find my birth parents and let them know how important their decision was; how it impacted my life, and thank them.

I had to thank my biological mother for her most difficult decision, one she had to bear alone: having me, then giving me up for adoption. I know this could not have been easy and impacted her life with so many regrets until we met.

I met them all, and learned my biological parents both moved on in life, having their separate families. I have six biological siblings too; we have now integrated and known each other for twenty-one years now. It's been such a blessing to be part of their children's lives, too.

> *Life is a song - sing it. Life is a game - play it. Life is a challenge - meet it. Life is a dream - realize it. Life is a sacrifice - offer it. Life is love - enjoy it.* -Sai Baba

Traumas from my childhood have held me back. They are

deep in my subconscious and I have to bring these shadows to light. If I don't, they will always be there. I have learned that all they do is weigh you down whether you know it or not. I might not even know they are there, they are so deep in my subconscious, just because they are so deep, doesn't mean they are not there, so by writing, all of a sudden what comes to light is like going to a therapist, it's a great way to get there.

The moment you do this you will start regaining your alignment and gaining your confidence. The more I associate myself with my inner voice and soul, the better. Fear is the reason in the majority of times we do nothing in our life. Fear leads to uncertainty because of constant changes there are deep inner feelings of emotional thinking. This is not where I want to be, nor do you. It feels horrible, you feel frightened, fearful, uncertain, disappointment sets in, rejection and failure, and this holds us back, because we have not done this before. We have to realize we need to use our tools, ones we have at our fingertips to transmute that energy.

In order to change our lives, we have to think different thoughts, we cannot pay attention to what is, instead we need to focus on "where we are going," aim for the version "we want to become." We lose track when we focus on "what is." It keeps us in the wrong energy. We often think it's okay because we've been in it for a long time and don't really care, but when we leave ourselves, settling for less, it means we are settling for everything in life.

You need to listen to our own inner guidance; you want your actions and thoughts to align with that which comes from your inner self. Huge growth and change come from transforming yourself. That's why it's important to be your genuine authentic self, let yourself shine, be you, the way you want to express yourself, dress, let your hair down, no people pleasing, "do you," shine and lead by example!

If you don't you will look up at the "what is happening" instead of "what you want it to be." You will make fearful choices, you will be in constant indecision, carrying emotions from the past in your body; being constantly led by trauma, you pay the wrong attention to the past pain, yet, you have to find a way to deal with this. Don't think for one minute that this is an easy road; however, it is important to go through the process.

When in an environment that brings traumas to the surface, know it will help you heal and that it is coming up so you can become present in your life.

If we are not present, we stay stuck in our fears and taking on more burdens than necessary because we are in this emotional state, we end up saying yes to people because we are feeling we are not good enough and we don't have a voice inside of us, we don't say, this is enough and too much, we just keep going, never getting out of this game of "life and works." We need to change our thoughts to become a better person within, we cannot keep speaking this negativity to ourselves. What we choose for ourselves must be what we want to become.

If you change your energy, you start opening your doors and realigning yourself for the better. You have to love what you are doing; look at the bigger picture or you will not attract the person you want to become. You have to go through this experience to reach where you want to be.

We all need to be the best version of ourselves, open ourselves up and provide it to the world; we have one responsibility: living our future preferably in a happier state, which is our birthright!

Back to the conversation with my discouraged friend...

I was so excited to let her know how far my journey had taken me and could not wait to share all the inner work that I have had to do to start changing my life for the better.

I was excited to share with her that I had just written a story, by co-authoring in an anthology book, collaborating with 21 co-authors in a book called, *A Note to my family, I am your legacy.* I explained how this transitioned my life once again by writing my story from my past to my present.

When asked if I would like to participate in this volume of *Rattled Awake,* instantly twenty-four years of emotions and pain burst through me like a metamorphosis! There's a transformational process that takes place, like a "caterpillar turning into a butterfly," affecting my thoughts, mind, and soul. Writing about it struck me straight in the heart like a dagger; it impacted me more than I ever realised…how long I had been carrying these feelings without realising it! By writing this chapter, I cried and released so much pain, which is now opening doors to healing,

I said yes!! to finally facing what was so needed. – Michelle Laaks

It's only when we truly know and understand that we have a limited time on earth - and that we have no way of knowing when our time is up, we will then begin to live each day to the fullest, as if it was the only one we had. - Elisabeth Kubler-Ross

I had discovered that I had a past and future life, and found a way to integrate both my family and my biological family in the course of writing this chapter. I suddenly realised the importance of helping those in the same situation, from both sides of the 'fence;' how I could help inspire and help so many in adoption scenarios.

It is during our darkest moments that we must focus to see the light. -Aristotle Onassis

This was my long overdue Rattled Awake moment, a huge 'aha' lit with passion! My purpose became clear as a bell: help others going through stuck moments of adoption and to live life with no regrets, too!

Even more, supporting their story through my "Art with heArt" and a deep understanding of their journey, assistance in writing their own story, inspiring others to walk the path so they may have no regrets, too, is an immense blessing!

I can relate my friend's story to my biological mom's story, and how important it was that I know I helped her have no regrets in life.

I came to realise my friend cannot leave this world without sharing her story. She was sure to let me know that since our meet up, she is thrilled to have started writing her story and wants me to illustrate it.

Inspiring others by acting in a positive light can help determine a better outcome. Doing what is right, from your values and heart, is so important. Based on all the feedback I've been getting from other people, I've got to do this…it is my mission!

Writing in these books has helped me the most if only by getting this out, sharing my message with others and through inspirational speaking, others are living life with No Regrets!

Accept the things to which fate binds you, and love the people with whom fate brings you together, but do so with all your heart. -Marcus Aurelius

Learning how to accept the unexpected and make the most of it is an important lesson that can help us to grow and to become better versions of ourselves.

Get your message out to the world and inspire others along your journey! Create legacies and be sure to leave this earth with No Regrets!

Life is what happens while you are busy making other plans. - John Lennon

I would be honored to help you through your self-discovery

journey, inspire you to never give up, and share your story by providing expertise in all these ways:

Storytelling - Editing - Publishing - Ghostwriting - Illustrations

When I stand before God at the end of my life, I would hope that I would not have a single bit of talent left, and could say, 'I used everything you gave me.' - Erma Bombeck

Michelle Laaks is on a mission to make a difference to help others in their lives. She knows the pains of adoption, and she knows how to help others create books so they can have their say. She gives people a voice and does that as an illustrator and co-author of international anthology books. She creates custom artwork design in all forms. Michelle is adept at capturing the moment and the emotion as well as the brand vibe in ways no one else can. She has shared her personal story of re-inventing her life for the focus of creating legacies and having No-Regrets, and is excited to speak to audiences as an inspirational and transformational speaker. You can find her on LinkedIn at **https://www.linkedin.com/in/michelle-laaks-52458932**

RATTLED AWAKE

"Over the past 5 years, what is the single biggest event that caused you to completely change your perspective for the better?"

We have all been impacted by dramatic shifts in life as we knew it to be. Who have we become as a result of these events?

These authors share one response in common: they became better, not bitter. And now, they are sharing their aha's with you in quick-read articles, in this ongoing anthology project.

Rattled Awake: Volume One

"Over the past 5 years, what is the single biggest event that caused you to completely change your perspective for the better?"
The first in a series, Rattled Awake is proud to present these 11 life-changing stories of how one incident dramatically shifted each of these authors lives' for the better:
You're never too old to rewrite your next chapter and change up your script ~Chef Jill Sullivan
Still So Much Life to Live ~Chris Freer
Not a "Cougar" or a "Karen" and Worth WAY More than 9 Pence... ~Erika Warfield

Transfer your Setbacks into Remarkable Comebacks. ~LeeAnna Stock-Luoma

Look Beyond the Box, For We Are So Much More ~Susannah Dawn.

Beneath the Perfect Score: The Silent Crisis of Student Suicides in Asian Cultures ~Dr. Constance Leyland

The Bipolar Pen: Unleashing the Gift of a Writer ~Nicole Angai-Galindo

Live Your Purpose Now! ~Russ Hedge

Growing With The Flow..~Willie J.

The Pressure Cooker ~Lonnee Rey

It's All an Illusion. ~Steve Kidd

Rattled Awake: Volume Two

No matter what has happened over the past five years, allow optimism enter. Each "Rattled Awake" moment can bring you a gift. Enjoy the treasures each author shares so freely here, and let them inspire you to rewrite your next chapter.

Lesley Mouton...That Ain't No Genie in a Bottle!

Bob Witty...This Has to Stop: A True Story About Veteran Suicide

Jill Sullivan...Caretaking for Grandma Joan, "The Candy Lady"

Doug Thompson... The Universe's Storyteller

Brian Schulman... You Are the Light in the Basement

Nancy Debra Barrows... Becoming

Gene Petrino... From Apathy to Action: Unleashing the Warrior Within

Michaela Riordan Turner, PsyD... Daddy Rocks!

Chiyedza Nyahuye... Miracles on the Playground

Willie J.... Surviving to Thrive
Niki Bell...Mastering Mysticism and Prevailing!
Lonnee Rey... This Bugs Me

Rattled Awake: Volume Three

Over the last 5 years, what single event rattled you awake? We have all been through a lot, especially in the last five years. What shook you?
These eight authors have eight uncommon experiences to share as they show you what it was like to pivot, improve and prevail. All of them shifted with the changing tides, becoming better, not bitter, and bring you nuggets of wisdom mined from the depths of their souls. enJOY!

Dare to Surrender...Lisa Marree
She's All HeArt...Michelle Laaks
Rising from Within...Dr. Nhu Truong
Grow Through...Wendy Wiseman
Laugh, Play, Heal...Chiyedza Nyahuye
Gremlins...Kim Groshek
Bend, Don't Break...George Monty
The Art of Traveling Light...Lonnee Rey

Rattled Awake: Volume Four

"Over the past 5 years, what is the single biggest event that caused you to completely change your perspective for the better?"

We have all been impacted by dramatic shifts in life as we knew it to be. Who have we become as a result of these events?

These authors share one response in common: they became better, not bitter. Driven to share their legacy message of hope and inspiration with you, they gathered together over one weekend to write their hearts out - to leave you feeling uplifted, perhaps a bit introspective and motivated to move beyond self-limiting concepts.

The FOURTH in a series, Rattled Awake is proud to present these 7 life-changing stories of how one incident dramatically shifted each of these authors lives' for the better:
Doma Nunzio...Find the Others
Brian Luoma...Quite the Fish Tail
Tonya Davis...Letting Go to Grow
Wendy Wiseman...Slow Your Roll
Dr. Michaela Turner...I Solve a Problem
Lonnee Rey...Untying the Knots

AN OPEN INVITATION

The "Rattled Awake" movement is an ongoing series dedicated to promoting messages from everyday people on a mission to share their legacy, in print, forever.

The writing workshops continue to inspire both first-time writers as well as experienced writers - all of whom benefit from the collaboration as well as the training.

If you have ever wanted live coaching and help getting your thoughts down on paper, then out into the world, this is your chance.

"Don't die with the music still in you." Dr. Wayne Dyer

Write one chapter - in one weekend - and enjoy the status "Co-author of the Best Seller, Rattled Awake" forever.

Visit OfficialRattledAwake.com for more information about the next workshop.

Schedule a chat with Lonnee Rey - together, you can hone-in on how to convey your Rattled Awake moment.